Improving Executive Sponsorship of Projects

Improving Executive Sponsorship of Projects

A Holistic Approach

Dawne E. Chandler
Payson Hall

BUSINESS EXPERT PRESS

First published in 2017 by
Business Expert Press, LLC
222 East 46th Street, New York, NY 10017
www.businessexpertpress.com

ISBN-13: 978-1-63157-411-5 (paperback)
ISBN-13: 978-1-63157-412-2 (e-book)

Business Expert Press Portfolio and Project Management Collection

Collection ISSN: 2156-8189 (print)
Collection ISSN: 2156-8200 (electronic)

Cover and interior design by S4Carlisle Publishing Services
Private Ltd., Chennai, India

First edition: 2017

10 9 8 7 6 5 4 3 2 1

Printed in the United States of America.

Abstract

This book is a resource for senior managers looking to enhance project outcomes by improving executive project sponsorship. It is also a source for project managers and sponsoring executives seeking information to improve sponsor effectiveness.

Improving Executive Sponsorship of Projects addresses gaps in current project management literature. From a senior management perspective, the gap is the lack of resources explaining why and how to establish a program to improve executive sponsorship strategically across an organization. From a tactical perspective, the gap is a scarcity of actionable materials to clarify roles, responsibilities, expected behaviors, and identify support necessary for improving sponsor effectiveness.

The authors identify key factors to consider before creating an executive sponsorship improvement program or enhancing an existing one and explain why executive sponsorship is important to an organization, how an organization's culture influences the effectiveness of the sponsor role, and why project management standards are critical to success. They explore what roles, responsibilities, and behavior should be considered and how to determine whether the person in the sponsor role is the right person and prepared to do the job. Finally, the book provides a process, with tools, to assess an organization's readiness to implement an executive sponsorship program, develop a plan for improvement, and monitor the progress of a program once it has begun.

Keywords

executive leadership, executive sponsorship, organizational preparedness, portfolio management, program management, project management, project manager and sponsor relationship building, project sponsor behaviors, project sponsor training, project sponsor roles and responsibilities, project sponsorship, project sponsorship effectiveness, project sponsorship assessment, projects and strategic alignment, strategy, sustainability of project management, value of project management, value of project sponsorship.

Contents

Acknowledgments

We want to thank our respective spouses, Doug and Mardell, for their continuing support throughout this project and to Tim Kloppenborg for his encouragement to write this book. A special thanks to Randy Englund, Cheryl Kananowicz, and Tom Kendrick for their thoughtful reviews and helpful comments.

Preface

A credible modern book about sponsorship needs four ingredients that are hard to find in a single individual:

1. An executive who has implemented sponsorship in the real world on a national scale (depth—Dawne)
2. A consultant who has worked with a variety of organizations of different sizes and industries to implement and refine sponsorship programs (breadth—Payson)
3. An academic who is familiar with recent literature and the evolving role of the project sponsor (book learnin'—Dawne)
4. Someone who can communicate ideas clearly and concisely in writing (at this point we both point nervously at one another and look at the ground)

Dawne and Payson bring a combined 80 years of work experience to this book project, our complementary background and skills combining (we hope) to bring you a unique and useful reference. Although we have known each other since meeting in the mid-1980s when Dawne was the IBM marketing representative to Payson's start-up software development firm, our professional relationship blossomed 10 years later when Dawne was an executive for a multinational project-based organization where Payson's consulting firm was hired to teach project management and sponsorship.

Dawne has walked the talk. She built a PMO and served on the executive team of an organization for which effective project management and sponsorship were vital strategic disciplines. Over the course of 7 years, she introduced and sustained continuous improvement of project management standards and sponsorship practices. Retiring in 2012 to complete her doctorate in Organization and Management with an emphasis on project management, she complemented her advanced studies with practical experience of someone who has been there and done that.

Payson Hall began his project management career working on software development and later large-scale systems integration projects where profitability and project management are inseparable. Payson started a project management consulting and training company in 1991 that became Catalysis Group in 1993. Over the past 25 years Payson has helped a variety of public and private sector organizations improve their project management and sponsorship practices.

Troubled by the scarcity of material on how to improve the effectiveness of project sponsorship, Dawne was passionate about developing practical guidance that was actionable. This book project was born from a conversation between Dawne and Tim Kloppenborg in 2015, in which Tim suggested Dawne write her own book, combining her academic research and her real-world experience. When Dawne mentioned the project to Payson over lunch in the summer of 2015, he begged her to let him participate, firmly believing that sponsorship is the vital, underappreciated cornerstone of improving project management practice, and knowing that there was not much practical material about the subject in print.

Writing a book is hard work. We are pleased to say that our friendship has survived this collaboration, driven by our passion for the subject. We hope that you find the results helpful.

CHAPTER 1

Approach to Improving Executive Project Sponsorship

Defining Executive Project Sponsorship

An executive project sponsor is a senior manager serving in a formal role given authority and responsibility for successful completion of a project deemed strategic to an organization's success. Executive project sponsorship is the application of skills and political power to perform the role of executive sponsor and guide a project to successful completion. Successful completion is achieved by either meeting the project's defined goals or by terminating the project if its value proposition becomes compromised.

The Approach

This book, *Improving Executive Sponsorship of Projects: A Holistic Approach,* provides a resource for senior management, executive project sponsors, Project Management Office (PMO) leaders, and project managers seeking to improve the effectiveness of executive project sponsorship. Written from an executive's perspective, the book addresses the scarcity of material concerning organizational barriers to effective sponsorship and the necessity for senior management engagement in planning for and successfully implementing this role. From a tactical perspective, the book provides an approach for formalizing clear roles, responsibilities, and support, to improve sponsor effectiveness and working relationships with project managers. From a strategic perspective, the book offers a practical approach for engaging senior management in discussions about executive project sponsorship and the continuous improvement of this role. From an operational perspective, this book provides assessment tools to determine organizational preparedness for a sponsorship program and prioritize continuous improvement endeavors. This work focuses on the commitments that senior executives must make to position the executive project sponsor role to be successful:

- Ensuring linkages between projects and strategic initiatives
- Securing organizational buy-in to the role
- Implementing project management standards
- Defining clear executive project sponsorship roles and responsibilities
- Funding and supporting executive sponsorship training
- Ensuring the right people are in the role
- Planning for continuous improvement

We identify key factors to consider when creating or enhancing an executive project sponsorship program, explaining why executive sponsorship is important to an organization, how organizational culture influences the effectiveness of the sponsor role, and why project management standards are critical to sponsor success. Using a systems thinking[1] approach that looks holistically at the linkages and interdependencies between the components of a sponsorship program and its whole, we provide processes and tools for assessing the current state of organizational preparedness for executive project sponsorship and developing a plan for improvement and monitoring progress. Finally, we offer practical suggestions for improving communication between project sponsors and project managers, a keystone to success.

This chapter first asserts the value of executive project sponsorship, and then traces the evolution from ancient to modern thinking about sponsor roles and responsibilities and explains why senior managers are crucial to this role. Next we review traditional sponsor responsibilities during the project life cycle. The chapter concludes by introducing the framework used in Chapters 3 through 6 to guide development of an

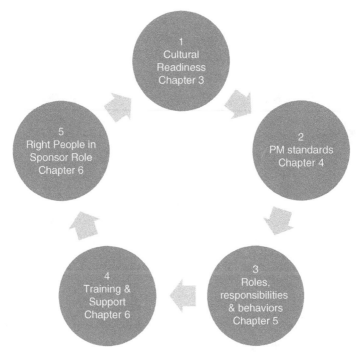

Figure 1.1 Framework for assessing a sponsorship program

executive sponsorship improvement plan (Figure 1.1) and highlights an organizational preparedness assessment tool for monitoring continuous improvement (Figure 1.6) explored in detail in Chapter 7.

Executive Sponsorship

In its 2016 publication of executive leader and PMO director survey results, the Project Management Institute (PMI) reported projects with active executive sponsorship were more successful than those without it (Figure 1.2).[2]

Executive project sponsorship can have a profound impact on project success and is a strategic role that requires thoughtful implementation and careful nurturing. The ideas and concepts in this book will help shape thinking on how to approach sponsorship program development and implementation to make it more effective and provide a path for continuous improvement.

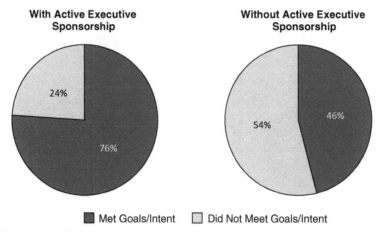

Figure 1.2 Projects with and without active executive sponsorship

Origins of Executive Sponsorship

History provides insights about how the project sponsor role has evolved over time. Project executive sponsorship has existed in some form for millennia. Consider the great projects of antiquity, when kings like Khufu of Egypt sponsored architectural wonders like the Great Pyramid at Giza in 2500 BC.[3] Since the beginning of recorded history powerful rulers and religious leaders have served as sponsors, commissioning engineering masterpieces throughout the Greek and Roman eras, Chinese dynasties, and the European Renaissance.[4] Notable project sponsors are visible throughout the 1800s during the Industrial Revolution and the 1900s in numerous landmark projects. Each of these historical projects had some form of executive sponsorship, represented by the person(s) who oversaw or championed the efforts to successful completion. In these instances, the sponsors provided leadership by supplying funding, ensuring resources were available, and using their political power to overcome barriers. Figure 1.3 depicts some of these notable historic sponsors. The function of these historical sponsors is similar to the roles of the project sponsor found in the recent literature.[5]

Modern Conceptualization of Executive Project Sponsorship

As the project management discipline became more formalized in the latter half of the 20th Century, the need for better definition of the project

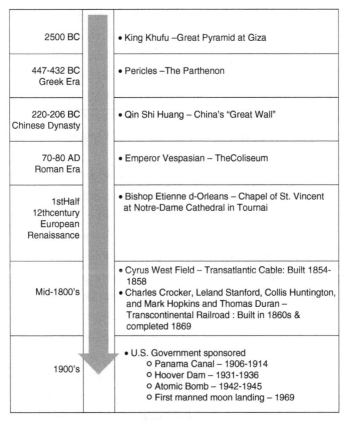

2500 BC	• King Khufu –Great Pyramid at Giza
447-432 BC Greek Era	• Pericles –The Parthenon
220-206 BC Chinese Dynasty	• Qin Shi Huang – China's "Great Wall"
70-80 AD Roman Era	• Emperor Vespasian – TheColiseum
1stHalf 12thcentury European Renaissance	• Bishop Etienne d-Orleans – Chapel of St. Vincent at Notre-Dame Cathedral in Tournai
Mid-1800's	• Cyrus West Field – Transatlantic Cable: Built 1854-1858 • Charles Crocker, Leland Stanford, Collis Huntington, and Mark Hopkins and Thomas Duran – Transcontinental Railroad : Built in 1860s & completed 1869

1900's	• U.S. Government sponsored
	    o Panama Canal – 1906-1914
	    o Hoover Dam – 1931-1936
	    o Atomic Bomb – 1942-1945
	    o First manned moon landing – 1969

Figure 1.3 Some notable historic sponsors

sponsor's role became apparent. There was an emerging understanding of project managers as responsible for day-to-day planning, management, and execution of projects, but this duty could not be performed in a vacuum. Members of the senior management team had an essential role in funding, guidance, oversight, and representing an organization's interest in project decision making. Initially, "sponsor" was defined primarily in relation to project management practices. The 2000 edition of PMI's *A Guide to the Project Management Body of Knowledge (PMBOK® guide)*[6] uses the word "sponsor" fewer than a dozen times in the body of the document, generally describing the sponsor as a funder and approver of key deliverables, risks, and changes. Until late in the 20th Century, little was written about the characteristics and responsibilities necessary for effective sponsorship or how to do the job.

Over the past 20 years, executive sponsorship has become recognized as critical to project success. No longer just a figurehead for oversight and approvals, the executive sponsor has become an integral member of the project team with more clearly defined role and responsibilities. A synopsis of these pivotal years provides insight into the emerging behaviors identified as necessary for effective sponsorship and project success.

A review of project management literature from 1997 to 2013 shows the term "executive project sponsorship" gaining momentum.[7] From 1997 to 2006, research focused on identifying roles and responsibilities as well as:

- Behavioral attributes—enthusiasm, interest, ownership, reputation, seniority, influential power, communication skills, and compatibility
- Specific facets of the role—being a project's champion, financier, supporter, power broker, or relationship builder
- Commonalities to historical responsibilities—setting objectives, providing funding and resources, facilitating stakeholder communications, and promoting teamwork by motivating, recognizing, and compensating the project team[8]

Researchers began reporting sponsorship responsibilities in terms of their organizational context, like new product launches and complex infrastructure projects.[9] Phrases like "using positional power as an influencer" became associated with sponsorship along with an emerging emphasis on the sponsor serving as a coach and mentor to the project manager.[10] Sponsorship was discussed in the context of the sponsor's willingness to be available to the project team and the sponsor's role in assuring that the project being sponsored was an appropriate use of organizational resources.[11] Juggling multiple needs of various stakeholders and dealing with complexity and chaos became identifiable as key attributes of effective sponsorship.[12] As sponsorship evolved with the support of top-level management from managing projects to programs and then portfolios, interest grew in the application of situational leadership skills in project sponsorship.[13] By 2006 there was recognition that careful selection and assignment of an executive with specifically desired characteristics was more effective than simply assigning any available senior executive to act as sponsor on mission critical projects. A consensus emerged among thought leaders in the field that sponsors needed to exhibit additional attributes to be successful[14]:

- Willingness to drive change in the organization
- Capable of developing mutual trust relationship with the project manager
- Ability to take a holistic view of the project
- Diplomacy in dealing with peers and senior management
- Ability to establish and maintain discipline on the project
- Capacity to make timely and informed decisions
- Involvement and commitment throughout the project
- Passion for the project

Drivers were identified that positively impacted project sponsorship effectiveness, such as having visible support from top management, effective mechanisms for stakeholder communication, formalized roles and responsibilities, a level of sponsor involvement commensurate with the organization's commitment to the project, co-operation from peers, and compatibility between the sponsor and organizational values.[15]

Until the mid-2000s, no widely accepted model existed for determining who might best fill the sponsorship role. In practice the definition and implementation of the sponsorship role varied from one organization to the next. There were no published sponsorship role standards as there were for project managers.[16] However, evidence emerged showing there were consistent themes regarding how the role was effectively performed, which led to the creation of the Situational Sponsorship Model.[17] The Situational Sponsorship Model emphasized considering an organization's needs for project governance and a project's need for support, which facilitated a better determination regarding the skills and competencies required of a sponsor for a specific project. There was also recognition that effective sponsorship was dependent upon personal characteristics and behaviors of the individuals carrying out the role.[18] Three key behaviors highlighted were:

- Excellent communication and listening skills
- Effectively handling ambiguity—especially in complex projects and programs
- Managing self when faced with competing priorities

With the global economic collapse of 2008, investors demanded increased organizational transparency in operational activities. Assigning accountability for key strategic project initiatives to a senior manager was recognized as a desirable solution. The sponsorship role emerged as a focal point for ensuring accountability, transparency, and strategic implementation of project-oriented investment opportunities.[19] As no prior sponsorship role and responsibility model had existed, the Situational Sponsorship Model, published that same year, was well timed for organizations that needed tools to determine, refine, and clarify sponsorship roles and responsibilities.

Current Thinking on Sponsorship Roles and Responsibilities

As interest in sponsorship standards continued to grow, individuals from the private and public sectors worked together to create a framework and set of standards for assessing the performance qualifications and competencies for project sponsors.[20] The GAPPS (Global Alliance for Project Performance Standards): A Guiding Framework for Project Sponsors was issued in August 2015 to support organizations interested in developing sponsors through established standards for sponsor roles and responsibilities. This framework is a performance-based competency model that infers competency based on the assessment of personal attributes and performance. Some details of the model's elements are found in Chapter 5.

Today's Expectations for Sponsors

Despite the evolution of the role in practice and in literature, one might wonder, "Why all the buzz about project sponsorship, isn't it really just about doing the things management does to help shepherd a major initiative through to successful completion?" It is that, but much more. Industry's understanding of the duties and contribution of the position has evolved and become refined over time. It is no longer acceptable to be an "accidental project sponsor," one unaware of or incapable of supporting the organization's project management practices or fulfilling the expected roles and responsibilities of project sponsorship.

Research has shown that when project sponsors are actively engaged projects have a higher likelihood of success,[21] but what does active engagement look like? It means involvement throughout the project life cycle, capitalizing on a sponsor's seniority, insight, and experience to benefit the project team, whether breaking down barriers, negotiating for resources, mentoring, or providing timely decisions.

Table 1.1 outlines where and how sponsors are traditionally involved in the five major project life-cycle phases today. While local practices regarding sponsor roles and responsibilities may vary, Table 1.1 is an example of what has worked successfully for the authors in practice.

Table 1.1 Sponsor involvement activities by project management life cycle phase

Sponsor Involvement Activities by Project Management Life Cycle Phases				
Initiating	Planning	Execution	Monitor & Control	Close
Verify & maintain strategic alignment of the project with senior management				
▲			▲	
Meet with project manager to discuss project charter, key stakeholders and expectations				
▲			▲	
Mentor project manager throughout project life-cycle to build their leadership skills				
▲	▲	▲	▲	▲
Review and sign-off on project plan and significant plan changes				
	▲		▲	
Attend project kick-off meeting and explain importance of this project to the organization				
	▲	▲		
Meet with project manager to review project status				
▲	▲	▲	▲	▲
Review and provide feedback on risk register and high priority risk response plans				
	▲	▲	▲	
Review and approve change requests that alter project scope, schedule, cost, and quality				
	▲	▲	▲	
Attend regularly scheduled core team meetings, providing insight and support				
	▲	▲	▲	
Attend project close-out meeting for celebration and recognition of team members				
				▲

An Organization Must Tailor Its Approach

Whether an organization has an established and effective sponsorship program, is looking to refine or improve an existing one, or is just beginning to explore the benefits of implementing a more thoughtful approach to sponsorship, the first step is to determine how the role is performed today and how it might be more effective. Readers exploring this book for ideas should consider the following as they develop their plans.

First, there is no one "right" way to implement the executive sponsorship role and its associated responsibilities. Each organization must decide how they want to use sponsors, who best fits the role, and what roles and responsibilities fit the organization's business context.

Second, an organization's environmental factors must be considered to develop an approach and pace that are feasible. This book contains suggestions based on our experience, but plans must be developed mindful of the organizational history and context.

Third, build support for your initiative with the executive management team early and work to sustain it. The process, cultural, and behavioral changes required to build and maintain an effective sponsorship program are not huge, but they require buy-in, co-operation, and commitment from the highest levels of the organization to succeed. Fortunately, there should be early, visible returns on the program investment in the form of better communication, more informed decision making, and better project outcomes.

As we will explore in later chapters, we believe the secret lies in not overcomplicating sponsorship implementation. We encourage our readers to avoid making start-up or improvement plans onerous. Start small and grow practices organically, particularly if no existing structures are in place. If existing structures are inadequate, add to them gradually. In our experience, success requires identifying organizational roadblocks and eliminating them and then focusing on what is expected of sponsors, getting necessary training, and then executing the role with appropriate support.

Depending on where an organization is in implementing both project management and the sponsorship role, the five-step assessment process (repeated below as Figure 1.4) provides a framework for building and

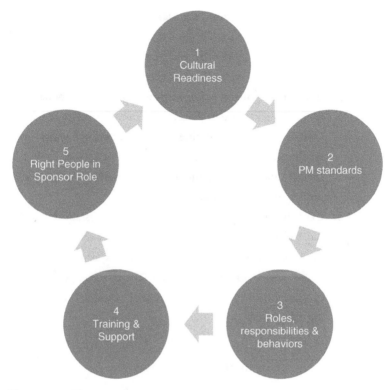

Figure 1.4 Five assessment steps

improving a successful program and the agenda for the remaining chapters. Each of the steps must be considered in turn and local practice/ performance brought to a minimally accepted level for each iteration of the process as part of the overall program. The steps are outlined below and explored in more detail in Chapters 3 through 6 along with guidance for assessing each area. Integrating those assessments to support initial planning and ongoing process improvement is described in Chapter 7. Planning for process improvement is addressed in Chapter 8.

Step 1. **Cultural readiness:** Gain buy-in from the senior management team that having executive project sponsors on key strategic projects is important for organizational success. Agree on what this role means to the organization and what culturally needs to be in place to support it.

Step 2. **Project management standards**: If an organization has minimal standardized project management practices defined and in use, then identify and implement a minimum useful set of practices to facilitate project success.

Step 3. **Executive sponsor roles, responsibilities, and behaviors**: Once standards are in place, define and formalize the sponsorship role, responsibilities, and expected behaviors. As a baseline, consider the list of sponsor activities from Table 1.1. Identify and communicate the sponsor behaviors expected to both sponsors and project managers.

Step 4. **Executive sponsor training and support**: Establish a training and mentoring program that supports sponsors in performing their role, responsibilities, and expected behaviors.

Step 5. **Right people in sponsor role**: Make effective performance of the sponsor role a key component of evaluating sponsoring executives.

Chapter Overviews

The remainder of this book describes an approach for building or refining an executive sponsorship program customized to the needs of an organization. Each chapter begins by explaining why the material is relevant, then exploring the material in detail. Chapters conclude with discussion questions and considerations for PMO and Project Management staff. For each element of the framework in Figure 1.4, assessment tools are provided in Chapters 3 through 6. If this book is used in an academic setting, the discussion questions can be used to stimulate learner debate and/or assess their knowledge in a particular area.[22] Figure 1.5 lists the book's chapters.

Chapter 2 explains why executive project sponsorship is important to an organization and why putting plans in place to improve or start a sponsorship program improves the chances for project success. The contents of Chapter 2 may be helpful in gaining buy-in from executive management for the sponsorship program.

Chapter 3 discusses how an organization's culture influences sponsorship and explores whether an organization is currently positioned to

Chapter 1
- Approach to improving executive project sponsorship

Chatper 2
- Executive sponsorship matters

Chatper 3
- Cultural influences on executive sponsorship

Chapter 4
- Importance of project management standards

Chatper 5
- Desirable executive sponsor characterisitics

Chatper 6
- Sponsor readiness

Chatper 7
- Roadmap to organizational preparedness

Chatper 8
- A plan to enhance executive sponsorship

Chapter 9
- Summary

Figure 1.5 Overview of the book

support the executive sponsorship role. A set of cultural assessment questions and a tool for gauging cultural readiness are provided.

Chapter 4 discusses the value of project management standards and practices to an organization. A set of tools recommended to support effective sponsorship and questions for assessing existing project management standards are provided.

Chapter 5 explores behaviors and temperaments necessary for effective executive sponsorship and explores current thinking on sponsor roles, responsibilities, and performance criteria. A collection of scenarios is presented to highlight necessary sponsor actions and rationale. The GAPPS *Guiding Framework for Project Sponsors* is presented and discussed as a foundation for gauging current sponsor competencies and an assessment tool is presented for examining individual sponsor behaviors.

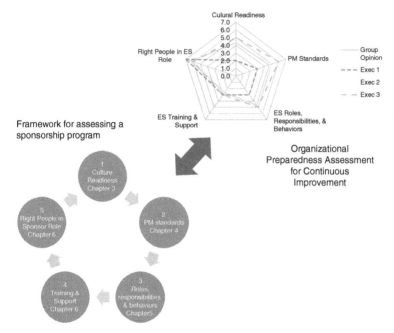

Framework for assessing a
sponsorship program

Organizational
Preparedness Assessment
for Continuous
Improvement

Figure 1.6 Assessment framework interaction with organizational preparedness tool

Chapter 6 explores the readiness of assigned individuals to perform the sponsor role. It provides assessment tools for gauging the effectiveness of an executive sponsorship program by examining project outcomes, and also examines existing sponsor training and support programs with an emphasis on preparing individuals to serve in the sponsor role.

Chapter 7 provides the organizational preparedness assessment (Figure 1.6) tool for consolidating assessment data gathered using the tools in Chapters 3 through 6. The overall assessment facilitates developing and prioritizing initial improvement plans as well as monitoring ongoing improvements to the executive sponsorship program.

Chapter 8 outlines a holistic approach for incorporating the material from previous chapters into an action plan for improving executive sponsorship and offers recommendations about initial priorities for organizations with minimal sponsorship infrastructure.

Chapter 9 summarizes the book's key take-away messages and encourages a call to action to begin the journey for improving executive project sponsorship.

Questions for Discussion

1. Projects throughout time have had sponsors—what new information has emerged in the early 21st Century regarding the sponsorship role that has changed expectations?

2. Why might sponsorship and standardized project management processes depend on one another for success?

3. Although more detail is presented later in this book, what factors were identified in this chapter as important to planning a sponsorship initiative?

4. What environmental factors might help or hinder development or enhancement of a sponsorship program?

5. Why might assessment and continuous improvement be important to a sponsorship program?

Considerations

Project Management Office

The PMO has an opportunity to take a leadership role in helping senior management understand the organizational importance of the executive sponsor role and in assessing the health of the organization's sponsorship program. PMO staff insights can be valuable in shaping the roles, responsibilities, and behaviors of sponsors and identifying the training and support required. The PMO should be prepared to provide senior management with the data needed to assess and build an effective sponsorship program.

Project Manager

Experienced Project Managers have an opportunity to offer their insights and vision for improved sponsorship roles, responsibilities, and behaviors. Actively engaging in dialogue with senior management as executive sponsorship is refined not only helps the project manager gain confidence working with executives but also affords them a unique opportunity to see an executive's perspective of the role as it is being transformed.

Notes

1. Peter Senge. 1990. *The Fifth Discipline: The Art & Practice of the Learning Organization,* (New York, NY: Doubleday).
2. Project Management Institute. 2016. *PMI's Pulse of the Profession: The High Cost of Low Performance,* (Newtown Square, PA: Author), p.13.
3. Mark Kozak-Holland. 2011. *The History of Project Management,* (Oshawa, ON, Canada: Multi-Media Publications).
4. Ibid.
5. Bryde, 2008; Chandler, 2013; Crawford et al., 2008a; Helm and Remington, 2005; Kloppenborg, Tesch, and Manolis, 2011; Kloppenborg et al., 2006; and Walker and Dart, 2011.
6. Project Management Institute. 2000. *A Guide to the Project Management Body of Knowledge, (PMBOK® guide)* (2000 ed.).
7. Blomquist and Müller, 2006; Bryde, 2008; Christenson and Christenson, 2010; Cooke-Davies, 2005; Cooke-Davies et al., 2007; Crawford et al., 2008a; Hall, Holt, and Purchase, 2003; Helm and Remington, 2005; Hydari, 2012; James, 2011; Kloppenborg, Manolis, and Tesch 2009; Kloppenborg, Tesch, and Manolis, 2011; Kloppenborg et al., 2006; Padar, Pataki, and Sebestyen, 2011; Pinto, 2000; Sense, 2013; Sewchurran and Baron, 2008; Tighe, 1998; Whitten, 2002; and Wright, 1997.
8. Cooke-Davies, 2005; Hall, Holt, and Purchase, 2003; Helm and Remington, 2005; Kloppenborg et al., 2006; Pinto, 2000; Tighe, 1998; Whitten, 2002; and Wright, 1997.
9. Hall, Holt, and Purchase, 2003; Helm and Remington, 2005; and Tighe, 1998.
10. Kloppenborg et al., 2006; Pinto, 2000; Hall, Holt, and Purchase, 2003; Helm and Remington, 2005; and Tighe, 1998.
11. Crawford, Pollack, and England, 2006.
12. Hall, Holt, and Purchase, 2003.
13. Cooke-Davies, 2005; and Blomquist and Müller, 2006.
14. Labuschagne, et al. 2006.
15. Cooke-Davies et al. 2006.

16. Project Management Institute. 2007. *Project Manager Competency Development Framework,* (2nd ed.), (Newtown Square, PA: Author).

17. Crawford et al. 2008b, p. 76.

18. Ibid., p. 67.

19. Crawford et al. 2008a, p. S43.

20. GAPPS. 2015. *A Guiding Framework for Project Sponsors,* Sydney, Australia: Global Alliance for Project Performance Standards, accessed October 5, 2015, http://globalpmstandards. org/downloads.

21. Bryde, 2003 and 2008; Cooke-Davies et al., 2006; Christenson and Christenson, 2010; Crawford et al., 2008a; Kloppenborg, Tesch and Chinta, 2010; Kloppenborg, Tesch, and Manolis, 2011; and Sewchurran and Barron, 2008.

22. Kloppenborg and Lanning, 2012, p. 13.

CHAPTER 2

Executive Sponsorship Matters

All projects need sponsors to serve the role of "owning" the project outcome and working with the project manager to control the project boundaries and provide management support and perspective for key decisions. Smaller, simpler, less significant projects may have the sponsor role filled informally by line or functional managers. As projects become more complex and more important to an organization, sponsors become more critical for project success and sponsor responsibilities grow. The most important projects or programs gain tremendous advantage from having a senior executive formally assigned to serve in the role of executive sponsor. This chapter explains the importance of executive sponsorship and how executive sponsorship improvement programs increase the chances of project success.

Executive Sponsors Improve Project Visibility

Projects or programs that align with strategic initiatives are more visible. When a project is on senior management's radar, the likelihood of project success increases because visible projects are more likely to get the resources and priority needed.[1] One critical resource that improves visibility is an effective executive sponsor.

Historically, it was common practice for executives to establish strategy and then delegate implementation to lower-level management.[2] In the world of strategic projects, however, executive sponsors are an integral part of the implementation team, playing a vital role in daily project activities, helping the effort stay on track and providing advice and tactical decisions as project needs arise. Sponsors also continue to serve their strategic role by providing insight regarding the project's direction, while serving as a communication bridge between the project and the executive team.

When senior management appoints an executive sponsor to a strategic project, it assigns accountability for successful implementation to an individual with the authority to influence the outcome. Research shows that high-performance organizations that actively engage sponsors have a higher percentage of projects meeting their goals.[3] Having a peer directly accountable for project success provides the executive team the benefit of unfiltered communication about a project's progress and significant barriers encountered. Senior management expects the sponsor will keep them informed as well as proactively seek advice on significant risks or risk responses. This steers sponsor behavior toward engaging senior management when appropriate, rather than shielding them from project information.

Prioritizing Projects for Executive Sponsorship

All projects should align with an organization's strategic goals; however, even aligned projects may not always receive needed resources. Resource allocation is complex and imprecise, and there are often essential operations as well as strategic projects competing for the finite resources available. Prioritization of needs and appropriate and effective allocation of resources to address them are two of management's most formidable challenges.

A similar prioritization process occurs when determining which projects require an executive sponsor and allocating an appropriate executive to the role. This sponsorship prioritization process should normally occur as part of strategic planning and portfolio management. There are a limited number of executives with the competencies and skills needed to effectively sponsor projects and not every executive is ready to perform sponsor duties. Chapter 5 discusses the competencies and skills required of sponsoring executives. For now, let us examine how to determine which projects have the greatest need for executive sponsorship.

Executive sponsors are normally reserved for projects that address strategic initiatives and significant projects that are highly complex. One approach to executive sponsor assignment is to prioritize projects based on these two key criteria, the project/program's strategic alignment and complexity. Projects in the high-complexity and high–strategic alignment quadrant are prime candidates for an executive sponsor assignment. Figure 2.1 is a graphical representation for sponsorship assignment with Project 2 and Project 9 demonstrating priority need for executive sponsorship.

Sponsorship Assignment to Emerging Projects

Projects sometimes arise that were not anticipated during strategic planning. The strategic alignment or complexity of a project may also change or evolve into a higher quadrant that warrants reconsideration. An ad hoc nomination process is helpful to enable any executive within an organization to champion and nominate a project for sponsorship when the situation warrants. Senior management is served in this case by pre-establishing

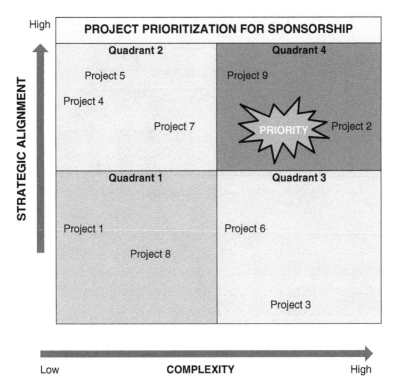

Figure 2.1 Prioritizing projects for executive sponsorship

criteria for triggering sponsorship assignment. The criteria must fit the organization, be adapted to the business needs, and senior management should collectively agree beforehand on the situations that require executive sponsorship. Candidate criteria to consider include:

- Does this project significantly address one or more strategic initiatives? Which ones and how?
- Do the strategic benefits of this project warrant special executive involvement? Why?
- Do identified project risks warrant special executive involvement? Why?
- Does the complexity of the project warrant special executive involvement? Why?
- Has the organization successfully completed projects of comparable scope, schedule, and cost before?
- Does the project involve co-ordination with multiple organizations (internal or external)?
- Does implementation involve multiple sites, regionally, nationally, or globally?
- Is a significant new product or service being created?
- Does the effort involve implementing significant new technology?
- Is the effort addressing or subject to regulatory requirements that are complex or time sensitive?
- Will the project result in significant organizational change affecting the organization, its customers, or business partners?

A project that triggers one or more of these criteria may be a candidate for executive sponsorship. Consider a project that incurs substantial financial penalties if contractual deadlines are not met; assigning a sponsor to help keep the project on track may be prudent. If the situation does not fit defined criteria, then the executive champion will need to present a compelling rationale to prioritize the effort for executive sponsorship.

The project's executive champion, who may or may not ultimately be the assigned sponsor, presents the case to the senior management team requesting an executive sponsor be assigned. In today's context, the executive champion is typically referred to as the person who believes in the project's intent, wants to see it succeed, and advocates for authorization and initiation for the project to begin. Figure 2.2 is an example of a process for nominating a project for executive sponsorship. Although all projects should have a designated sponsor, qualified executive sponsors are often in short supply. Only the most critical projects warrant an executive sponsor assignment.

Having standardized project prioritization and sponsor nomination processes in place ensures a thoughtful approach to prioritizing which projects require an executive's time and attention. If a Project Management Office (PMO) exists, it can facilitate this process. If not, the administrative roles and responsibilities noted in Figure 2.2 can be assigned to the executive team's staff. Once criteria are established, the nomination process structures information that senior management wants to consider to streamline the discussion. Figure 2.3 is an example of an executive sponsorship nomination form customized to use some of the criteria above. Note on the form that the championing executive presenting their request for an executive sponsor may be suggesting an executive other than themselves based on that person's unique competencies and skills to handle the challenges of this particular project/program.[4] Following the presentation, senior management will discuss and decide whether the project/program warrants executive sponsorship and determine the best person to assign depending on the executive sponsor candidate's availability and capability.

Advocating that executive sponsors be reserved primarily for high-priority and complex projects is not to say that lower-priority

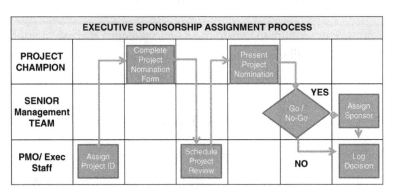

Figure 2.2 Executive sponsorship assignment process

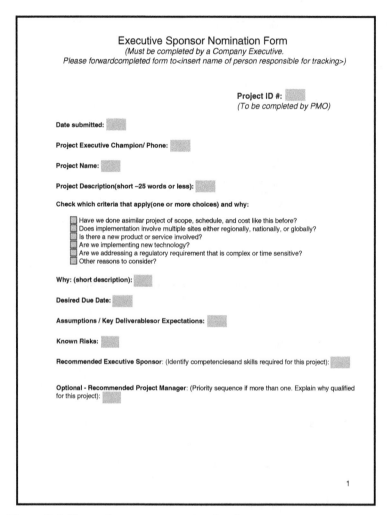

Figure 2.3 Executive sponsor nomination form

projects do not require sponsorship. All projects require effective sponsorship and, as we will see, sponsorship assignments are essential for a project and good for the skills and career development of sponsors.

Leadership Development

An Opportunity for Executive Development

The sponsorship role can be leveraged to develop and enhance executive skills. Project sponsor experience helps develop and refine leadership, communication, negotiation, and mentoring skills. Sponsorship training and work experience can be integrated into each executive's development plan to encourage engagement and participation.

Functional executives with minimal cross-functional or matrix management experience will find that serving as a project sponsor for an enterprise-wide project exposes them to new challenges. They will have opportunities to gain leadership experience and insight by interacting with other functions in ways they may not have previously because of siloed responsibilities or newness to the executive role. In the sponsorship role executives are responsible for ensuring smooth co-ordination across multiple functions where they may have little prior exposure. Effective sponsors learn to seek the perspectives of key stakeholders. They practice perfecting their leadership and communication skills when interacting with groups with differing perspectives and goals. The importance of earning trust and respect, giving clear and decisive direction, and the gratification that comes from motivating others to support the project are all lessons available to an attentive sponsor. Projects can also be a crucible for learning different aspects of a business as a result of building new cross-functional relationships. When managing a cross-functional project, executives have ample opportunity to polish their negotiation skills by collaborating with functional managers, clients, and vendors to obtain and maintain adequate project resources and eliminate barriers to progress.

Sponsorship provides an opportunity to develop and enhance mentoring skills. Mentoring the project manager is a key responsibility that allows the sponsor to pass along valuable organizational knowledge to help guide project manager decisions and help the project manager and project succeed. From our personal observations, one of the most important things a sponsor can do is cultivate a trusting relationship with the project manager so the project manager will communicate with the sponsor without fear of reprisal. When a project manager is uncertain or confused, this confused state is critical information that should be shared, not hidden. Building and sustaining the bond between the project manager and sponsor is key to open communication and learning for both. Sponsors must remember that project managers do not have exposure to organization-wide decisions that might impact their projects; thus, the more context and insight an executive can provide, the more prepared the project manager can be to manage project risk and changes and frame decisions in a business context.

Professional development opportunities from sponsorship also exist for senior executives. Two key reasons to consider the most senior executives for sponsor assignments are:

1. They know how to get things done
2. Their stature means others are likely to watch and follow their lead.

Senior executives can set an example and often be the best teachers for other executives to learn and emulate how the sponsorship role should be performed. When executives are shown how sponsorship influences project success they become ambassadors for the practice. Teach sponsors how project management standards are used to manage projects, clarify their roles and responsibilities, and provide the support needed to perform their role, and executives are more likely to support project management maturation in the organization. As junior-level executives and project managers typically aspire to work closely with senior staff, the sponsor role is an excellent way to infuse purposeful mentoring responsibilities into the most senior executive's development plan.

An Instrument for Future Leader Development

Project sponsorship can be used to develop future leaders for an organization. By training potential leaders in standard project management practices, sponsor roles and responsibilities, and assigning them to sponsor projects appropriate to their skill level, leaders learn by doing.

Start inexperienced sponsors with smaller functional projects, and then graduate to more complex cross-functional projects as individuals demonstrate their competencies and develop their skills. To groom someone for promotion to the manager rank, consider assigning them to sponsor a modest project. Someone being considered for a Director-level position might be assigned to sponsor a more substantial project that crosses multiple functional groups.

Successful sponsor assignments can be a gateway to management promotion. Each assignment provides opportunities to demonstrate the qualities sought in a manager: leadership, negotiation, organization, communication, and mentoring skills. Sponsorship not only tests candidates' capabilities but also gives them invaluable on-the-job training before putting them in their new role. Observing a candidate performing the sponsor role on a cross-functional project provides an excellent opportunity to see how they handle responsibility before putting them in an executive role where they are expected to sponsor more mission critical endeavors.

A Mechanism for Project Manager Development

Inexperienced project managers typically are not comfortable or adept at conversing with upper-level management, particularly senior management outside of their immediate organizational boundary. Whether attributable to the sponsor's rank and influence, or the project manager's lack of confidence, the project manager often assumes that if the sponsor needs something they will ask. The power differential often results in a measure of intimidation. The sponsor needs to help the project manager feel comfortable that the sponsor can be trusted and must find ways to build a relationship with the project manager such that the project manager feels comfortable initiating sometimes difficult conversations and believes the sponsor is there to help.

An example of a learning moment between sponsor and project manager that helped build a trusting relationship:

Building a Trusting Relationship

An executive sponsor shared concerns that the project manager was not meeting frequently enough with him to keep him apprised of project status. The project management standard adopted by the organization dictated that the project manager was to meet at least monthly with the sponsor and more frequently if needed. When asked if the project manager had discussed meeting monthly with the sponsor, the sponsor said yes and at the time he had thought that was adequate. As the project progressed, the sponsor became frustrated that he was not being briefed more frequently. The sponsor admitted that he had not

---

(Continued)

Building a Trusting Relationship (*Continued*)

shared this frustration with the project manager. When asked why, the sponsor said he felt the project manager should have asked him. The recommendation was that the sponsor speak to the project manager about his concerns and ask for more open and frequent communication between the two. The project manager was told there was a communication frequency problem with the sponsor. She was surprised and did not realize there was a problem. The project manager met with the sponsor and they agreed to meet more frequently and things improved.

Lesson learned—the project manager thought the frequency of updates was adequate but the sponsor did not and was not sharing his concern. When they started talking and agreed to have more open communications, a relationship formed that was not only beneficial for the project but to both individuals as they learned to take more proactive steps to ensure each was getting what they needed. At the close of the project the sponsor rated the project manager's performance highly and requested her frequently on future projects. Trust was built and a mutually beneficial relationship was formed.

Executive Sponsorship Encourages Investment in Project Management

We have seen clients make significant investments in project management practices, realize the benefits of those practices, and then allow their project management programs to atrophy over time because organizational memory did not recall the value project management provided (Figure 2.4). It is challenging, expensive, and time consuming to develop and socialize good project management practices.

How can an organization keep project management value forefront in senior management's mind to encourage sustained investment? Research shows that leveraging executive sponsorship is a very effective mechanism.

Until recently the impact of executive sponsorship on the sustainability of project management within the organization was not supported with scientific evidence. New research shows that when executives serve

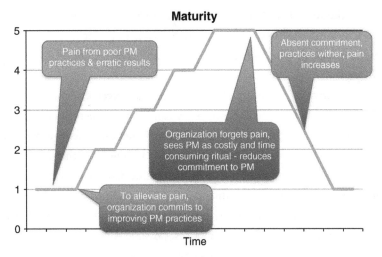

Figure 2.4 Waxing and waning commitment to project management

as project sponsors there is an increased likelihood they will continue to invest in project management because of their perception of the value the organization receives.[5] A correlation was found between senior management's likelihood to continue to invest in project management when sponsorship roles and responsibilities are clearly defined and formalized and training occurs. When neither of these happens, executives show no inclination to value or invest in project management. Figure 2.5

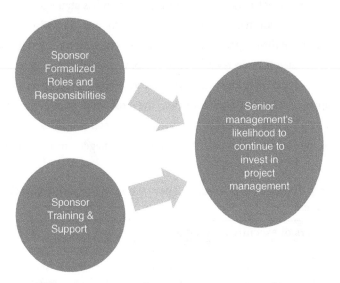

Figure 2.5 Executive sponsorship impact on continued investment in project management

depicts the influence that executive sponsorship has on the likelihood that senior management will continue to invest in project management when formalized roles and responsibilities and training and support are provided.

If executives are unaware of the value they are receiving from project management then the likelihood for continued investment will be low. For organizations that are on a path of implementing effective project management practices, it is important to leverage resources that reinforce positive perceptions of project management value. Continued investment can be seen in terms of recruitment dollars for qualified project managers, training funds for sponsors, project managers and team members, top-down support for effective practices, possible support for a separate PMO, and recognition for project success.

Research has identified three key influencers of executive management perception concerning project management value and the likelihood of continued investment (Table 2.1)[6]:

First, the more experience an executive has with sponsorship the more likely that executive will see value and continue to invest because they gain a better understanding of how to leverage project management practices for project success. This can be encouraged by providing sponsorship training to all executives and actively engaging them as sponsors. Second, the higher the project management maturity level an organization has attained, the greater the likelihood senior management will continue to invest in project management because of their experience that the use of consistent tools and processes produce better-run projects and better outcomes. Third, the more seasoned the executives, the more likely they are to see value from project management. Seek support for sponsorship efforts from the most senior management levels.

A low project management maturity level presents a chicken-and-egg problem; an organization with a low project management maturity does

Table 2.1 *Influencers of executive perception of the value of project management*

Influencers of executive perception		
Number of times an executive performs the sponsorship role	Organization's project management maturity level[7]	Years of senior management experience

not have project management processes and tools in place to clearly demonstrate the value of project management to senior management. Without demonstrating value, it is difficult to sustain momentum to evolve a program to higher levels of maturity. The best hope for low-project management maturity level organizations to survive is to obtain support from senior executives who understand the value project management promises in the medium to long term and who are willing to support the effort as it matures. One of the best ways to garner senior executive support is to engage them as sponsors. This provides an opportunity for those executives to see the value of project management first hand and increases the likelihood of their sustaining the investment necessary to achieve sufficient maturity to realize consistent benefits.

Summary

Executive sponsorship matters because it provides visibility to key projects to ensure alignment with strategic goals and encourage allocation of necessary resources. Sponsorship offers a mechanism for developing leadership skills in executives and future leaders and encourages investment in project management because of the perceived value executives see from using project management practices to execute projects more successfully. In Chapter 3, the influence of organizational culture on executive sponsor success is explored.

Discussion Questions

1. Why align projects to strategic initiatives?
2. What role does executive sponsorship play in improving project success rates?
3. What benefits are there for establishing project eligibility criteria for sponsorship assignment? Why is it important to prioritize projects for sponsorship assignment?
4. What are some ways to leverage the executive project sponsorship role for purposes of leadership development?

5. The relationship between the project manager and project sponsor is critical to project success, but the power differential between the roles can be a barrier to effective communication. How might problems in this relationship manifest themselves? As a sponsor, what might you do to address this potential problem?

6. How does executive sponsorship influence an organization's continued investment in project management?

Considerations

Project Management Office

Where a PMO exists, one of its primary strategic roles is to work with senior management to build and maintain clear priorities of the projects in the enterprise project portfolio. Priorities among projects facilitate efficient and appropriate assignment of limited resources. Skilled and effective executive sponsors are a particularly scarce resource, and the PMO can facilitate the assignment process by working with the executive team to establish criteria for project prioritization and management assignments to projects.

Project Manager

Establishing a trusted communication channel between the project manager and project sponsor is critical to project success. This can seem contrary to the pervasive myth that good project managers get projects done "no matter what it takes." Communication channels can be difficult to build and sustain if sponsor availability for dialog is limited or the communication is undervalued. In the real world on complex and mission critical projects there will be occasions where there are no good options available to the project manager. Building and maintaining trust and a basis for candid discussion about concerns, problems, and risks is essential to providing timely and accurate status reporting and seeking help or guidance promptly. The time to build this communication channel is before you need it. We encourage at least monthly informal conversations with the project sponsor one-on-one in a casual setting such as over coffee or lunch to discuss current status, concerns, risks, issues, and possible responses. A casual setting helps overcome some of the barriers inherent in the power differential between the project manager and sponsor and encourages candor. Building rapport and gaining experience with the sponsor's goals and thought processes helps project managers frame and fulfill their role as trusted advisors and lieutenants.

Notes

1. Randall L. Englund and Alfonso Bucero, A. 2015. *Project Sponsorship: Achieving Management Commitment for Project Success,* (2nd ed.), (Newtown Square, PA: Project Management Institute).

2. Kloppenborg and Laning, 2012, p. 2.

3. Project Management Institute. 2015b. *PMI'S Pulse of the Profession: Capturing the Value of Project* Management, (Newtown Square, PA: Author), p. 9.

4. David West. 2010. *Project Sponsorship: An Essential Guide for Those Sponsoring Projects Within their Organization,* (Burlington, VT: Gower Publishing Company), pp. 20–21.

5. Dawne Chandler and Janice L. Thomas. 2015. "Does Executive Sponsorship Matter for Realizing Project Management Value?" *Project Management Journal,* pp. 46–61.

6. Chandler and Thomas, 2015, pp. 53–54.

7. Project management maturity levels — "The foundation for achieving excellence in project management can best be described as the project management maturity model (PMMM), which is comprised of five levels . . . . Each level represents a different degree of maturity in project management" (Kerzner, 2004, p.193). Level 1 — Common Language, Level 2 — Common Processes, Level 3 — Singular Methodology, Level 4 — Benchmarking, and Level 5 — Continuous Improvement.

CHAPTER 3

Cultural Influences on Executive Sponsorship

This chapter sets the stage for a senior management discussion about organizational culture and how well the management team is positioned to support the role of executive sponsor.

The Influence of Culture

Effective project management and sponsorship together can provide a competitive edge by improving project execution—provided the organizations where these practices are implemented have a culture that supports and encourages the kinds of decision making and change that project management enables.

Contrary to a great deal of marketing hype over the last 20 years, project management is NOT a magical "silver bullet" that enables all efforts to finish on time and on budget with exceptional quality work products and happy customers. Project management is much more mundane; it is a set of practices that try to facilitate understanding of the work to be done, anticipate and address challenges and risks, monitor execution, and support timely decision making when problems and opportunities arise. To nurture and benefit from the information provided by project management, the organizational culture must be willing to receive and act upon that information promptly—whether or not the news is pleasant.

Is the Enterprise Ready for Project Management?

All organizations engage in projects of some kind. Any effort outside the routine of day-to-day operations to develop or revise a product or service or make some significant change to the work environment or customer experience is a project. Examples include new product development, procuring and furnishing a new facility, developing and launching a new marketing/advertising campaign, and significant upgrades to work processes or infrastructure.

Most organizations need to see the benefits of project management before they are willing to escalate their organizational commitment to the processes and discipline. Fertile ground for a project management improvement initiative is an organization that consciously engages in projects and recognizes and seeks opportunities for process improvement.

Culture can enhance or discourage the evolution of more effective project management processes, and must be honestly assessed to determine whether an organization is ready to support an initiative to improve executive sponsorship and how to prioritize the effort. Consider the following questions:

1. Has the organization had successful experiences using cross-functional teams?
2. Are roles and responsibilities on cross-functional teams generally clear and respected by team members and functional managers?
3. When something goes wrong, does the organization prioritize looking for lessons learned and making process changes to avoid repeating the mistake, or affixing blame and allocating consequences to individuals involved?
4. Does the management team generally trust and support one another?
5. Does the management team tend to treat one another with courtesy and respect even when they disagree?
6. Does the organization have established project management practices and standards in place? (More on this in Chapter 4)
7. Are projects generally defined, planned, and managed consistently with standardized project management practices?
8. Does the organization consciously allocate resources to tactical daily operations as well as more strategic long-term efforts, or are nonoperational projects pursued with whatever effort is left after daily operations have been addressed?

9. Do people assigned the role of project manager in the organization have formal training in project management or do they tend to learn on the job?

10. What proportion of the executive staff has received formal project management training?

11. How many of the executives have formally served in the role of project manager during their careers?

12. Does the organization have a strategic plan that is current and actively referred to when considering new initiatives and priorities?

13. Does the strategic plan include metrics to track progress toward accomplishing objectives?

14. Does the organization maintain a list of significant projects currently underway?

15. What metrics are actively tracked and reported at the executive level for strategic projects?

16. How are significant proposed changes to a project's budget, schedule, or scope agreed upon and documented?

17. When significant projects complete, do they proceed through a formal close-out process? Does that include a final report to the executive team?

18. Does the organization provide time-tracking mechanisms to monitor individual hours performed on projects?

19. Does the organization provide accounting methods to allocate costs to specific projects?

20. Do executives believe project sponsorship is a major part of their job and that they have time to devote to it? How many hours of an executive's time do they estimate are directly related to projects underway?

Few organizations have the organizational and project management maturity to answer all of these questions favorably, and a few unfavorable responses are merely indications of cultural barriers to be considered as part of the organizational change necessary to implement executive sponsorship. If, however, an organization is feudal, authoritarian, blaming, rejects standard practices, avoids strategic planning, has a haphazard approach to project definition and tracking, and the executive team is already overworked, there may be higher priority issues to pursue than trying to implement an executive sponsorship program.

Cultural Pitfalls

An anthropologist friend once described culture as "the unspoken and unwritten rules about how a group behaves and interacts." Her definition is sufficient for our purposes. Although culture is a multi-faceted concept, there are a few key cultural attributes that correlate with project management effectiveness in our experience.

After exploring the 20 questions above to better understand how culture influences project management effectiveness, utilize Table 3.1 as a first step for assessing a culture's general support of project management. Subsequent chapters will provide additional assessment input on cultural readiness by delving more deeply into standards, roles and responsibilities,

Table 3.1 Cultural attributes that correlate with project management worksheet

Cultural Behavior/Orientation	Favorable ⟵⟶ Unfavorable	
1. Blaming—Are mistakes and failures openly discussed without fear of reprisal?	Usually	Rarely
2. Business Orientation—Are teams aware of project business value?	Usually	Rarely
3. Embrace of Process—Are appropriate processes encouraged?	Usually	Rarely
4. Collaboration—Do cross-functional teams play nicely together?	Usually	Rarely
5. Response to Risk—Is discussion of risk encouraged?	Usually	Rarely
6. Flexibility and adaptability[1]—Does the organization actively engage in process improvement and innovation?	Usually	Rarely
7. Theory X/Y—Does the organization seek and value the perspective of the troops on the ground?	Usually	Rarely
8. Executive Transparency—Is the rationale for decision making discussed with staff?	Usually	Rarely

adequate training support, and a process for selecting the right executives for the role.

A given organization will find its typical cultural behavior for a given attribute on a continuum of maturity somewhere between the extremes. If many of the attributes are in the unfavorable zone, it suggests significant cultural barriers to an effective sponsorship program. We explore our rationale for each attribute's impact on project management effectiveness below.

1. Blaming

    Perhaps the biggest barrier to effective project management is what is called a "blaming culture."[2] In a blaming culture all significant errors are quickly allocated to one or more individuals who are then punished for their transgressions. The first question asked in a blaming culture is "Who?" not "Why?"

    Blaming culture runs contrary to the project management goals of transparency and accountability. When a project is not going well or when a significant risk is realized, effective project managers should quickly analyze the situation, promptly notify the project sponsor, and execute appropriate risk response. If the project manager fears for his or her job whenever there is a problem (and there WILL be problems), this will discourage the timely and accurate flow of information essential for effective executive decision making. One of our client executives underscored the importance of timely and accurate delivery of bad news with a pithy sign on the wall over his desk. It read, "Around here we don't shoot the messenger . . . Unless he's late."

2. Business orientation

    Effective sponsorship and project management depend upon a project initiation process that identifies the project's business value. Project teams that understand the value propositions of their projects are better prepared to identify and assess threats to that value, opportunities to improve value, and trade-offs that should be considered or avoided.

    When business objectives are unclear or business value is not shared with the team, we have observed individual team members tending to exhibit two types of behavior: (1) Focus on the tactical—ignore the value proposition and do what they are told, to the best of their ability without a business context; or (2) make assumptions—guess at the business context and use the resulting assumptions to drive decision making and recommendations. Neither of these behaviors are ideal. Both result in increased likelihood of errors and diminished involvement of the team.

3. Embrace of process

While the process improvement pendulum often swings between embracing rigor and avoiding it,[3] there is a place in every organization for some standardization of processes where it makes business sense.[4] While some organizations in our experience appropriately debate the specific costs and benefits associated with a proposed new or changed process, others seem more inclined to a knee-jerk reaction that rejects process as unnecessary or restrictive.

Activities that are complicated, repetitive, and high risk/high value often benefit from process standardization as a way to improve consistency of performance and incorporate lessons learned. The aviation industry provides an excellent example of this principle.[5] Modern airline pilots do not improvise the processes they use to prepare for takeoff and landing of commercial passenger jets, because missing a step can mean disaster. The motor vehicle industry provides another illustration through standardized placement of controls in an automobile cockpit, allowing a driver to casually move from one vehicle to another without specialized training.

Process standardization can also result in productivity gains. Standardization of project status reporting, for example, allows project sponsors to quickly change contexts from one project to the next without having to reorient to each individual project manager's reporting style.

4. Collaboration—Do cross-functional teams play nicely together?

Some cultures are more collaborative than others. Complex projects that cross organizational boundaries, such as new product development, which might require assistance from engineering, manufacturing, contracting, sales, marketing, and support organizations, can be challenging under the best of circumstances. In organizations where communication and co-operation across organizational boundaries is limited, implementing a complex project is nearly impossible. Improving collaboration across organizational boundaries requires executive leadership and support and is a prerequisite to effective management of cross-disciplinary projects.

5. Response to risk—Is discussion of risk encouraged?

Many organizations launch projects with the unreasonable assumption they *cannot* fail to achieve defined goals. Even when projects are well defined in terms of schedule, scope, and resource goals, it may not be apparent to sponsors and key stakeholders that there are threats and barriers to achieving these goals. Unfortunately, it is difficult for many people to talk or think about possible threats to success without fearing that they will be perceived as "being negative." As a consequence, acknowledging risk and potential for failure becomes a blind spot in many organizations. Because an organization is unable to see or discuss potential problems, there may be little or no interest in risk management. The irony is that discussing and planning for risk can raise awareness and potentially protect projects from unknown threats.

As an illustration, instructors in military paratrooper school focus primarily on things that could go wrong during a parachute jump. They communicate expected risks: trees, power lines, rivers, and parachute failure, and have troops drill appropriate responses to these risks *while still on the ground*. Since they have discussed it, imagined it, and drilled for it, paratroopers are better prepared to react if something goes wrong when they are falling from the sky. Waiting for a parachute to fail before considering an effective response is a fatal approach to parachuting. Waiting for a critical project component to fail before considering an effective response is a fatal approach to projects. While it is easy to see the importance of risk planning before you jump out of an airplane, many organizations stubbornly deny the possibility that a project might not go as imagined.

Organizational taboos against failure ("Failure is NOT an option!") can present an even bigger barrier. In organizations with a taboo against failure, communicating information that may even hint at the possibility of failure is consciously or unconsciously discouraged. Honoring this taboo leaves project teams unprepared for risks and creates an environment in which problems are not communicated when they surface, but instead are ignored. Delayed communication about problems decreases the likelihood they can be dealt with effectively before they seriously damage the project.

If an organization has cultural taboos against discussing risks or admitting that projects might fail, it will be challenging to implement effective project and risk management processes and protocols. If risks cannot be surfaced, discussed, or planned for, why waste time with risk management? This attitude undermines the practice of proactively guarding against potential project threats.

6. Flexibility and adaptability—Is the organization dynamic and evolving?

   Much as some organizations may be resistant to new or changed processes, some organizations, particularly in established industries or the public sector, can become inflexible and resistant to change. While this disposition, unaddressed, can present a real threat to an organization's survival, it paradoxically also makes most remedies— such as a shift toward project management culture—more difficult. To be clear, all organizations experience some resistance to changes in how they operate—but beyond a point, resistance to new technologies and ways of doing business can be both self-limiting and destructive. Healthy organizations constantly evaluate ways to better adapt to changes in their environment, markets, and industries. If an organization resists innovation and evolution of its core business processes, how can it apply lessons learned?

7. Theory X/Y—Does the organization value and seek the perspective of its people?

   The prevalent management philosophy of the industrial revolution is often characterized by a somewhat rigid, hierarchical command and control structure referred to as McGregor's Theory X.[6] Under Theory X, workers are assumed to be unambitious, avoiding work and responsibility where possible, and motivated by pay or fear for their jobs. Theory X assumes that managers have most of the answers and that workers are best given clear direction and monitored closely.

McGregor's Theory Y is a competing theory that takes a more humanistic view of the workforce, assuming that workers are intrinsically motivated and generally take pride in their work. Theory Y presumes that the workers are more intelligent and have more to contribute to the conversation.

Modern complex projects often require input from diverse interests. While senior management may have a more strategic perspective, often the individual team members will have invaluable domain-specific knowledge and experience with similar efforts that can help identify the best approach to certain situations as well as risks that might pose threats to success. Organizations whose culture discourages soliciting and valuing input from individual team members and domain experts will find that this cultural perspective inhibits effective project management and problem solving.

8. Executive transparency—Are the rationale for decision making shared with staff?

"Because I said so" is the justification of last resort when arguing with a three-year-old, yet we have observed executives in some organizations who felt their authority was being challenged when asked about their motivation for project decisions. An organizational culture that does not share the thought process and justification for decisions and priorities creates three significant problems:

- Decisions seem arbitrary—which tends to undermine confidence in leadership, particularly if the decision seems to run contrary to common sense in the eyes of project team members.
- If the decision is based on bad information or incorrect assumptions the team has no opportunity to correct the executive misinformation before the decision is implemented.
- Even if the decision is right and proper, without understanding the thinking behind the decision, the project team is in no better position to anticipate the next decision.

Organizations whose culture sustains executive transparency wherever possible tend to be more nimble and also have staff who are better informed and better able to support executive decision making.

Each of these cultural attributes provides insights into whether an organization is ready for project sponsorship and helps to identify particular challenges that a program might need to address.

Ready for Project Sponsorship?

Executive sponsorship thrives when the organizational culture "allows" the sponsor to be effective. Sponsors are perceived to be effective when projects complete successfully and there are no complaints about their behavior. In preparation for planning a sponsorship initiative, here are some questions to consider:

- How can an organization determine whether it is enabling sponsors to be as effective as they could be?
- How would an organization know if it is ready to support executive sponsorship?
- How might problems be identified? For example, are sponsors getting the co-operation needed when it is needed? If not, why not?
- What are the causes of resistance and what can be done to make the environment more conducive to effective sponsorship?

Let us define organizational culture, in the sponsorship context, as "a shared set of beliefs that govern how people behave toward executive project sponsorship." In practice, one would look for evidence that the executive sponsor is supported by the organization. While public statements of support are helpful, support is better demonstrated by senior management action, for example, "walking the talk." Senior management encourages supportive behavior by engaging their teams and consistently indicating why the sponsor role is important, what the responsibilities and expected behaviors of sponsorship are, and how sponsors are held accountable for project success. It is not enough to say, "Sponsors are accountable." Teams must understand that accountability means the sponsor answers to the organization for project outcomes. This is demonstrated when teams see rewards and consequences for project success and failures. It is reinforced when senior management acts collaboratively to find workable solutions when sponsors ask for assistance. When interacting with sponsors, effective senior management models the supportive behaviors that it expects from the rest of the organization.

Further evidence that a culture supports sponsorship includes senior management creating an atmosphere that encourages open dialogue about the role and the interactions that occur between sponsor and project team. Senior management can define and actively support the sponsor role and listen to and address issues team members raise to demonstrate their commitment. Discussing and refining the sponsorship role based on team feedback is an excellent method for diminishing resistance and encouraging buy-in. As an example, we have heard comments like "We don't need sponsors because we have a project manager capable of managing that project". Clarifying how the roles are different and the expectations of each helps socialize sponsorship and build buy-in for the role.

The Problem with Believing . . .

"We don't need sponsors because we have a project manager capable of managing that project"

The roles of project manager and sponsor are fundamentally different. Project managers focus on tactical day-to-day aspects of the project. Sponsors worry about the project at a more strategic level and in the context of the entire organization. Project managers work with the team to identify potential risks and possible mitigation strategies, while the sponsor determines whether proposed mitigations are sufficient. Project managers seek to achieve the project goals as defined, and should not exceed agreed upon schedule, scope, or resource boundaries without sponsor consent. Sponsors establish the relative priorities among schedule, scope, and resources and serve as the voice of the organization if boundaries must be negotiated.

A key cultural indicator is how and to what degree an organization prepares sponsors for their role. Sponsors will be more effective if they possess the skills needed to perform the role and can demonstrate their competence. Sponsorship is a role ill-suited for a person who does not want the job, or who lacks knowledge about the organization's standard project management practices and the sponsor's role in them. A common belief we have encountered is, "Executives should just know how to be sponsors." The rationale being that sometime during their careers they may have led projects or they would not be at an executive level. The problem with this line of reasoning is that executives may or may not have recent and relevant project management or sponsorship experience.

The Problem with Believing . . .

"Executives should just know how to be sponsors."

There are many paths to the executive suite and some prepare new executives for sponsorship better than others. The ideal sponsor candidate will have had opportunities to serve in the project manager role on multiple cross-functional strategic projects working closely with, and being mentored by an effective executive sponsor. While this would constitute excellent preparation for serving in the role of executive sponsor, it is neither sufficient (there is more to learn) nor a prerequisite for the keys to the executive washroom. Many high-powered executives achieve their station because they are particularly good at finance, sales, or day-to-day operations. While their journey may have involved participating on project teams they may have little or no formal project management training or experience.

As we noted in Chapter 1, the project sponsor role has evolved rapidly over the past two decades. Sponsoring a project today brings new responsibilities and expectations not historically required of sponsors, such as active engagement throughout a project's life cycle and project manager mentoring. Executives also may not have managed or sponsored projects of significant scope. This leads back to the question, "How does the organization support sponsors to prepare them for this role?" Development and implementation of sponsorship training and assessments, as well as instituting professional development requirements for executives that encourage their growth in the sponsorship role are key cultural indicators of executive sponsorship support.

A foundation for executive sponsor success includes formalized training for both sponsors and project team members. This training must consistently describe the sponsor role, responsibilities, and expected behaviors as well as the collaboration expected between the sponsor and the project manager and project team members.

Other cultural clues to organizational readiness include evidence that sponsors are being regularly assessed on their performance, and that sponsor's professional development plans reflect adjustments indicated by their ability or inability to meet defined criteria for effective sponsorship (see Chapter 6 for an assessment process). It has been our experience that some executives are reluctant to participate in training and this is an organizational change challenge. The most common justification heard from executives who believe sponsor training is unnecessary is, "I already know what to do because I have managed numerous projects during my career".

The Problem with Believing . . .

"I already know what to do because I have served as project manager on numerous projects during my career."

Project managers are only positioned to see a fraction of a sponsor's duties. While defined interactions with the project management process are apparent, the negotiation, diplomacy, advocacy, and horse trading that an executive sponsor performs to support a project often do not occur within the view of the project manager. While a good sponsor might share highlights of these activities with a project manager he or she was mentoring, the shift in perspective from a project manager caring about the project to a sponsor caring about the project in the context of the organization's current mission and goals and future capacity can be jarring and surprisingly complex. Think of the project manager as a ship's captain—worried about day-to-day operation of the vessel, protection and timely delivery of cargo, and the safety of the crew. Contrast that with the concerns of a commander of a fleet of vessels—worried about all of the ships, but also needing to make and manage trade-offs among different ships to maximize short- and long-term profitability and long-term growth of the enterprise. Prior service as a project manager does not expose the new executive sponsor to all aspects of the sponsor role. This is part of our rationale for suggesting training be mandatory.

An effective training program establishes a common language and framework for all project participants regarding roles, responsibilities, and expectations. Full participation assures that everyone gets a consistent message and is essential for project success. Why do experienced executives and senior managers need to attend project management training?

Implementing or enhancing a project sponsorship improvement program is a significant organizational change undertaking. To the extent that the roles and behaviors of an executive sponsor are new or inconsistent with prior cultural norms, project team members will be understandably skeptical and they will closely monitor sponsor interactions for reinforcing or discouraging signals regarding the sincerity of the message. As an example, during project management training we seek to deliver a consistent message to team members and project managers that if they are unsure about what course of action to take when presented with a significant challenge, they should perform preliminary analysis and seek sponsor guidance promptly if confusion remains. People often perceive this approach as professionally risky behavior, because it admits to the sponsor that they are unsure how to proceed. In training, we assure teams that if they are unsure how to proceed, the sponsor wants to be apprised of the situation and may be able to bring additional forces or insights to bear on the situation. We encourage training participants to experiment with this behavior.

Is Sponsor Behavior Reinforcing or Undermining the Message?

Imagine that you are a project manager who has just attended training that emphasized prompt communication of problems to the sponsor. An issue has come up that has you and the team stumped. You see no viable responses that do not adversely impact either schedule or budget. The cultural status quo before the sponsorship program rollout would be for you to pick and implement the best option, then deal with consequences later when budget or schedule problems materialized. Mindful of the message of including the sponsor in such decisions, you tentatively approach the sponsor lay out the issue, and the sponsor says:

A. "Get out of my office! Don't come to me with a problem unless you have a solution."

B. "Thanks for bringing this to my attention. What have you thought of so far? What would you recommend? I am inclined to go in this direction . . . for this reason . . . does that make sense? Am I missing anything?"

Which of these responses reinforces the notion that cultural change is afoot? Which response suggests that nothing has really changed? An untrained sponsor can undermine the organizational change effort necessary for an effective sponsorship program in one or two episodes.

Establishing a culture that embraces and supports sponsorship is a challenging undertaking. Executive statements of intent to improve sponsorship are necessary, but insufficient on their own. Teams and executives will look for tangible evidence that cultural change is at hand and look for consistent behavior from their leaders. Leaders must actively lead by example to reinforce the cultural changes required for successful implementation.

Avoidable Sponsorship Deployment Pitfalls

Anticipate resistance when implementing an executive sponsorship program. We have seen resistance to the role play out in various forms and originate from different parts of the organization. It may come from executives themselves who find the role too demanding, line management that is not used to taking direction in a matrixed structure, or project teams that see the role as superfluous or confusing. Senior management can help address these three areas by setting the right tone and providing direction to subordinates, but when the executives themselves resist, it can be particularly challenging. Six common pitfalls to look for and avoid are listed below and explored further in the text that follows:

- Lack of buy-in
- Refusal to be trained
- Deficient competency or skills
- Poor performance not addressed
- Insufficient bandwidth
- Unsustained interest/focus

Lack of Buy-in

Senior management buy-in to sponsorship's value to the organization is critical. If one or more members of the senior management team do not value the role, there will be issues. This may express itself directly in lack of co-operation when a sponsor needs something from that executive or more subtly in the actions of the people who report to the unsupportive executive when they are assigned to a project team. It is essential to ensure buy-in rather than lip service from all executives before launching a sponsorship program. If the later behavior suggests buy-in issues are emerging, they must be addressed promptly. What follows is an example of what occurs when senior management has not fully bought in to the importance of the role.

The sponsor asks the functional executive who owns key members of a new product development project to use a standard reporting mechanism for their part of the project and to attend biweekly core team meetings. The functional executive refuses as he says the status reporting is not necessary because if someone needs to know how his team is progressing on their assignments they can ask him. He says he does not want to burden his team with keeping others outside their department updated. In addition, core team members from this functional group frequently do not attend core team meetings to discuss overall project status, risks, or changes to the plan. When asked about their absence, team members replied "if there is something the project manager thinks they must know then the project manager should reach out to them instead of making them attend a meeting." The cycle continues because the functional executive does not want someone outside his organization providing direction to his people. He wants to be known to his people as the one who protects them from unwanted or unnecessary work that others might ask them to do. Frustration levels rise and miscommunication thrives in this environment.

Refusal to Be Trained

Sponsorship training should be mandatory for all executive sponsors. Executives targeted for sponsorship assignments should not assume the role prior to successful completion of designated training. The goal of the training is to provide participants with a clear understanding of their roles and responsibilities as it pertains to executing the project management practices and the behaviors expected of them in this role. Soliciting feedback after the executives' training experience can reinforce these expectations. Questions to consider:

- What were the three things you learned that surprised you?
- What might you do differently after this training?
- How might training be improved to support you or others in this role?

These questions emphasize that training is important and reinforce key concepts. Some examples of what can occur when sponsors do not understand or fulfill their role and responsibilities during the project life cycle follow.

Leadership role: The project kick-off meeting is scheduled but sponsor does not attend, leaving the project manager to explain importance of the project to the project team when an executive-level perspective would have made a significant impact and provided greater insight.

Leader/Negotiator role: A cross-functional engineering and procurement team is doing the project for the manufacturing functional executive. The sponsor (also from engineering) instructs the project manager to handle the sign-off of all major project change requests saying she does not have the time, even though the manufacturing executive continues to ask for a number of changes, but expects the project to be delivered according to the originally agreed upon schedule. The project manager is left to manage/negotiate these changes with the manufacturing executive when the sponsor would most likely have more leverage and negotiating power.

Mentoring: The sponsor repeatedly cancels status meetings with the project manager and instructs project manager to keep him updated through email or call if something is needed. Project manager requests time to sit down and discuss some of the project's problems and get direction but the sponsor is unavailable. Lack of access leaves the project manager frustrated and forced to make critical decisions that would benefit from sponsor input. The consequence of leaving project managers to guess the sponsor's desires are decisions that may not reflect the needs of the business and a lost opportunity for project management mentoring.

Business decisions: The sponsor does not review or provide feedback on the high-risk response plans, leaving the success of the plan in the hands of the project team to analyze the plan and determine whether the planned responses are sufficient or if others need to make suggestions. The executive sponsor is uniquely qualified to weigh in on risk management issues because he or she has access to senior management and parts of the organization that may have experienced similar risk situations. Sponsor failure to engage with risk management is a lost opportunity to leverage the executive team's skills and connections, and the organization's experience.

Deficient Competency or Skills

How can an organization assure that the skills and competency of a sponsor are sufficient for the challenges of the role they are being asked to fill? An organization must pursue training, mentoring, and assessment of sponsors and assure that development plans prepare them for the challenging task of sponsorship. We have observed that sponsors who are not properly prepared face a variety of challenges. An example is described in the text box below.

POOR NEGOTIATION/DECISION MAKING—The project is behind because resources are repeatedly being pulled from the cross-functional team to support other initiatives. The sponsor has been ineffective in negotiating with peers and unwilling to change the scope of the project—put it on hold, or terminate it. Instead the sponsor instructs the project team to "Figure out how to do more with less and bring it in on-time." The issue is not that the resources are unneeded, the issue is the sponsor does not want to confront the other executive who is pulling the resources nor does he want his project to miss its delivery date which he believes will reflect badly on him. Instead of getting the help needed or making a decision to delay, he abdicates responsibility and pushes the problem back to project team. The consequence was a lot of frustration and overtime on the part of project team and late delivery of a substandard project work product. Different outcomes might have been available if the sponsor was skilled in the art of negotiating or willing to make difficult decisions about pausing or terminating the project. Other consequences: alienation of the team, staff turnover, breakdown in trust, and loss of executive level input into what trade-offs should be made among schedule, scope, and resources.

Poor Performance Not Addressed

Sponsor performance issues must be addressed when they happen. If necessary remove sponsors from the role until they have demonstrated they meet the criteria the organization expects. Do not allow an executive to "run rogue," ignoring all standards and expected practices. This causes friction between other executives when there is an expected level of communication concerning a project's status but one sponsor chooses not to provide it or when project teams expect sponsors to perform a role and the sponsor does not, leaving the project team without support.

Hiding the Ball—The sponsor tells the project team to keep risks internal to the project team and not include them in external status because the sponsor does not want anyone outside the team to know the project is in trouble. This goes against the standard practice of reporting all known risks and having response plans for high-risk critical projects reviewed by senior management. This directly contradicts a major effort underway to change the culture, encourage transparency, and let people know "We won't shoot the messenger of bad news." The sponsor is perpetuating the old culture and setting a bad example for the project team. This behavior undermines the objective of transparency, encouraging the opposite.

Insufficient Bandwidth

Most executives are not foolish or easily distracted, but they are often very busy. The executive sponsor role requires a commitment of time and attention that can be challenge for an already busy executive to fulfill. Projects that are going according to plan might require as little as 1 or 2 hours per week of a sponsor's time. What often begins as a minor time commitment can mislead executives to underestimate the amount of time required by the role and encourage them to budget insufficient time. When projects run into difficulties they often need significantly more attention from executives and may compete with other duties. Sponsoring a strategic project encountering significant difficulties can quickly become a nearly full-time job, putting executives in an untenable and uncomfortable position.

Spread too thin—An enthusiastic young executive eagerly sought the executive sponsor role for a strategic project as a chance to prove his worth. The project initially went smoothly and the executive added sponsorship of two additional projects to his other duties. When a business partner critical to two of the three projects he was sponsoring went bankrupt, the executive found himself unable to fulfill his duty to all three projects or adequately perform his other duties. Symptoms of the problem included:

- Executive working exceptionally long hours
- Projects receiving insufficient attention—missed meetings, slow decisions, slow response to email and telephone inquiries
- Performance issues and delays on other executive duties

Fortunately the executive's mentor recognized the problem and assigned sponsorship duties for one of the projects to another executive, then assisted the executive with the two remaining projects until the crisis had been worked through.

Unsustained Interest/Focus

Strategic planning can be focusing and energizing for an executive team. Looking beyond day-to-day operations to establish a clear direction and developing goals and tangible objectives toward achieving those goals is invigorating. The projects, programs, and initiatives that move the organization toward the goals may be exciting to launch, but can become mundane as they slowly unfold. Most sponsors take their duties seriously when a project is launched, but if a project continues relatively smoothly, some sponsors begin to take their role for granted and divert their attention to other activities. Alternatively, changes in the organization in the perceived value of a project may decrease a sponsor's interest. From a project perspective, the symptoms of a sponsor losing interest are similar to a sponsor who is spread too thin: missed meetings, delayed decisions, and slow responses to email or phone calls. A nonproject observer of the executive would notice a difference from the overwhelmed sponsor: a sponsor who is distracted or has lost interest in a project is generally not working excessive hours or letting their other duties languish. Active executive sponsorship is a cornerstone of project success. Sponsors who are no longer engaged with their project must be re-engaged or replaced promptly if the project is to succeed.

The massive mission critical program to implement an Enterprise Resource Planning (ERP) system had been actively sponsored for years. As different parts of the enterprise converted to the new system, the organization began to realize the long-awaited benefits. The finance department had initially sponsored the project and its lead executive served as the project sponsor. As the implementation grew, the organization created a new department to house the ERP operation going forward, and the project was administratively assigned to this new department. The executive sponsor now believed that the project had been operationalized and transferred to another organization. As a consequence, he pulled back from his duties. He began missing project meetings that he previously had led, although no new sponsor had been assigned. In the absence of active sponsorship, the project focus shifted from strategic (build this mission critical system correctly) to tactical (meet schedule commitments by trading off quality and functionality).

Assessing Cultural Readiness

Figure 3.1 highlights assessment areas discussed in this book that culminate in a framework for assessing the organization's overall preparedness to implement an effective executive sponsorship program. Collectively these assessments signal whether the organization is primed to support project sponsorship. It is not necessary that all elements are perfect for an executive sponsorship program to work, but establishing a baseline and then regularly assessing each subject area will help focus, prioritize, and continuously improve an organization's sponsorship program.

This version of the figure highlights the cultural readiness assessment that was the focus of this chapter. To assess cultural readiness, use the Chapter 3 material above and the 20 questions discussed earlier and engage senior management in a conversation about cultural readiness. Next, solicit senior management team impressions on the cultural attributes seen in Table 3.1 to establish a baseline. Typically it is a worthwhile exercise to allow each senior management member to individually score an

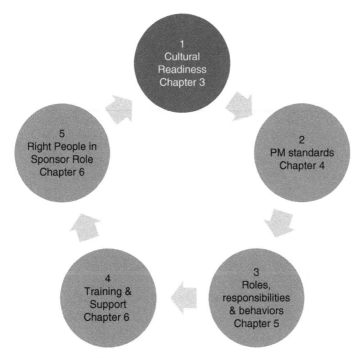

Figure 3.1 Framework for assessing a sponsorship program—cultural readiness focus

assessment area and then discuss the results with the group. This allows further group discussion and collaboration, leading to buy-in for creating an overall assessment score that will be used to measure continuous improvements. The cultural readiness assessment score will then be combined with other assessments as described in Chapter 7. The result will be an organizational preparedness chart in the form of a spider diagram that provides a snapshot view for continuous improvement efforts across all assessment areas discussed in Chapter 3 through 6.

The goal of the cultural readiness assessment is to determine whether the organization is mature enough to embrace the changes necessary to support an effective sponsorship program. The cultural readiness ideal for supporting executive sponsorship would be all parts of the organization consistently understanding and demonstrating:

- The belief that sponsors serve a legitimate and valuable purpose
- A clear definition of the sponsor role, responsibilities, and expected behaviors
- Support for sponsors serving in the role
- Respect and appreciation of sponsors for their contribution to project success
- Project outcomes are improved, but not guaranteed, by active executive sponsorship

This goal can only be achieved by an engaged senior management team modeling the behaviors they expect, establishing formalized roles and responsibilities, supporting and prioritizing training for sponsors and team members, and instituting a method for sponsor assessment that includes specialized training or mentoring to address performance gaps. These topics will be covered in subsequent chapters. Senior management's task is to emphasize and socialize the rationale for the sponsor role and demonstrate through their vision and actions that they believe sponsorship is integral to project and organizational success.

Discussion Questions

1. What are some of the impacts of culture on effective sponsorship?
2. What evidence might signal that an organization supports sponsorship?
3. What evidence might suggest areas where support for sponsorship needs improvement?
4. What are the pitfalls to avoid when implementing sponsorship and how might they be overcome?
5. What questions should senior management ask to stimulate dialogue about the organization's readiness to support sponsorship?
6. If organizational support is not present for sponsorship support, how might an organization close the cultural gaps?

Considerations

Project Management Office

The Project Management Office (PMO) can be a useful resource to senior management when looking to identify cultural barriers to project success. PMOs can provide insight to the 20 questions above and the questions in Table 3.1. The PMO may also possess or collect data on project and sponsor performance that is helpful.

When an organization seeks to modify its culture, the PMO can help socialize and reinforce the effort by realigning processes and practices to support the change. The PMO may also be in a position to provide discreet feedback during the change process if observed sponsor words or actions are inconsistent with the cultural shifts being promoted.

Project Manager

Project managers will have valuable insights into project and sponsorship challenges they have faced in an organization. They may also have a perspective on the 20 questions that senior management should consider. When asked to provide these insights, project managers should strive to be factual and not personal. Recommendations to overcome cultural barriers should be framed in a positive way. Rather than, "While serving as a sponsor, Mr. Jones made clear that he didn't want to hear bad news." consider, "I believe our organization would benefit from more open and timely dialog about issues and risks." Work with your PMO or with your peer project managers as a group to identify which questions are most appropriate for project managers to answer, for example, questions on teams, standards, roles, and responsibilities.

When organizations begin efforts to modify their culture, project managers have a particularly important role. Team members often look to the project manager for cues about whether attempted cultural changes are genuine or insincere and whether they are stalled or progressing. The leadership position of the project manager is key to nurturing early attempts at shifting the culture and encouraging patience and persistence as barriers are encountered along the way. The project manager can also provide direct feedback to sponsors diplomatically if sponsor words or actions might be perceived as inconsistent with stated organizational change goals. Project managers can have a big influence on the effectiveness of a cultural change initiative if they choose to support the effort.

Notes

1. Peter Senge. 1990. *The Fifth Discipline: The Art & Practice of the Learning Organization,* (New York, NY: Doubleday).
2. Gerald Weinberg. 1991. *Quality Software Management Volume 3: Congruent Action,* (New York, NY: Dorset House).
3. Lisa Bodell. May 15, 2012. "5 Ways Process Is Killing Your Productivity," *Fast Company,* accessed July 17, 2016, http://www.fastcompany.com /1837301/5-ways-process-killing-your-productivity.
4. Atul Gawande. 2009. *The Checklist Manifesto: How to Get Things Right,* (New York, NY: Metropolitan Books).
5. Matthew Syed. 2015. *Black Box Thinking: Why Most People Never Learn From Their Mistakes – But Some Do,* (New York, NY: Penguin Random House).
6. "Theory X and Theory Y," "NetMBA Business Knowledge Center," accessed May 22, 2016, http://www.netmba.com/mgmt/ob/motivation /mcgregor/.

CHAPTER 4

Importance of Project Management Standards

This chapter argues that establishing a common project management language and process standards is critical to the success of projects and a project sponsorship initiative. It provides a foundation for educating senior management about the value of project management practices and disciplines to an organization and encourages the investment necessary to implement project management processes.

A Common Language

According to the Project Management Institute (PMI) 2015 *Pulse of the Profession* study, 51 percent of high-performing organizations focus on standardized project management practices.[1] Compare that to the 14 percent of low-performing organizations with similar focus and a case can be made that standardized practices correlate with success (see Figure 4.1). This is consistent with our experience that standard project management processes, tools, and techniques enable an organization to more efficiently manage projects.

Standards establish a common language. A common project management language throughout an organization enables project stakeholders to communicate efficiently and sets clear expectations for roles and responsibilities. A baseline set of documented procedures allow the project manager to expect a certain level of performance from project team members in terms of understanding and adherence to the standard processes and tools used throughout the project life cycle. When team members arrive trained and familiar with common processes, tools, and project roles

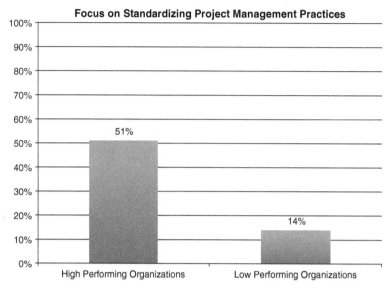

Figure 4.1 Utilization of standardized project management practices

and responsibilities, it frees the project manager from having to orient each project team member individually. If instead each project manager brought a unique set of tools and processes to each project, it would be inefficient and confusing for team members who work on multiple projects with different project managers.

Over time sponsors work with many different project managers and benefit from working in an environment with standardized processes and tools. Standardization allows the sponsor to more easily shift focus from one project to another and expect roles and responsibilities to be similar. Consistency enables the sponsor and project manager to focus on refining roles and responsibilities and adapting to the specific project context to build an effective working relationship rather than spending time identifying basic processes, tools, and techniques for managing each effort. In practice, we have seen the sponsorship role be more efficient when standards are in place. With competing priorities for an executive's time, baseline standardization enables efficient context switching without requiring orientation to each project manager's unique approach to common project management processes, tools, or techniques.

Essential Process/Tool Considerations

There are ample opportunities to develop and implement standard project management practices across the project life cycle depending on project management maturity, typical project size and complexity, and the unique business context and challenges facing a specific organization. Each organization must choose a baseline set of tools and practices, socialize and stabilize them, and then look for process refinements and improvements worth additional investment.

Although numerous sources propose a range of project management standards to help implement and sustain an effective executive sponsorship program, we have found the following five process/tool considerations essential for implementation. Each ties to the sponsorship roles and responsibilities highlighted in Table 5.1. Our priority considerations from a sponsorship perspective are:

1. Project life-cycle processes with associated sponsor engagement points
2. Communication Package
3. Meeting Minute Package
4. Risk management process
5. Change control process

Although details of designing and implementing a comprehensive set of project management practices are beyond the scope of this book, we encourage a systems approach[2] to process design and implementation and careful consideration of the organizational change implications of new or changed tools and standards. Planning for organizational change should be informed by systems thinking. Systems thinking is a holistic approach to problem solving that seeks to understand and balance the interactions between component parts with the whole of an organization. This approach is consistent with the presentation in this book, which recognizes the need to understand and influence an organization as a whole, rather than reducing change to the mechanics of modifying or enhancing the individual aspects. Chapter 7 discusses aggregating assessment data for the five key metrics of chapters 3 through 6, and Chapter 8 uses that data for prioritizing and customizing implementation planning, mindful of the influences of system thinking on the planning process.

In the balance of this chapter, we focus on critical linkages between sponsorship and the processes and tools necessary for efficiently and effectively managing the project and communicating with stakeholders. Processes should be built in consultation with stakeholders to secure buy-in. Where an organization does not currently have practices in place, initial tools and processes should favor simplicity and practicality to ease implementation. Keep early designs simple and refine them later with the benefit of experience. Explaining the rationale for each tool or process design and their organizational value is essential to gaining buy-in. The five areas we believe are most critical are explored in more detail on the following pages.

Project Life-Cycle Processes with Associated Sponsor Engagement Points

If an organization has few or no existing project management standards, it might wish to embrace the PMI's *A Guide to the Project Management Body of Knowledge (PMBOK® guide)*[3] as a framework for project management practices. PMI's five main process groups are initiating, planning, executing, monitor and controlling, and closing a project. Within each of these process groupings are key areas of engagement for the executive sponsor. When developing roles and responsibilities for the executive sponsor everyone must understand the processes for managing a project within the organization and specifically where sponsor engagement is expected. The project management process and standards are an essential component of the sponsorship training program. Aligning the sponsor roles and responsibilities to these five main process groups and defining when and how the sponsor must be engaged are critical to project success.[4] Table 4.1 is an example of sponsorship roles mapped to activities in the five project management process groups.

Communication Package

Numerous information exchanges with a variety of stakeholders occur throughout a project's life. We recommend a well-designed Communication Package to help the project manager keep diverse stakeholders with a need-to-know informed about project progress without generating countless individualized communications. If a single communication

Table 4.1 Sponsor touch points in a traditional project life cycle

Group	Activity	Sponsor role
Initiation	Charter development	Develop/approve
	Project manager appointment	Select/confirm
	Project definition	Consult/review/approve
Planning	Schedule	Consult/review/approve
	Budget	Consult/review/approve
	Scope	Consult/review/approve
	Project management plan	Consult/review/approve
	Proposed changes to the project definition*	Consult/review/approve
	Risks and risk plans*	Consult/review/approve
Execution	Emerging issues	Consult and resolve
	Emerging risks and risk plans*	Consult/review/approve
Monitor and control	Proposed changes to project definition*	Consult/review/approve
	Project status	Monitor
	Proposed changes to project approach*	Consult/review/approve
Close	Lessons learned	Consult/review/approve

*Change and risk management will be discussed in more detail later in this chapter and are included here for completeness

vehicle can be developed that meets the needs of diverse stakeholders it decreases the administrative burden on the project manager and facilitates efficient orientation and information exchange. Ideally the current version of the Communication Package is a single document that serves as the primary vehicle for communicating with stakeholders. Each section represents current-state information with the exception of the risk register and change control sections that aggregate historical information. Prior versions of the Communication Package serve as the project history.

- Project milestone status
- Key risks and risk response plans
- Change control log
- High-level solution diagram
- Statement of work (SOW)
- Key project core team and stakeholder contact list

The primary goal of the Communication Package is to facilitate and streamline communication between the project manager and the executive sponsor. Before examining the contents of the proposed package further, let us review the nature of sponsor/Project Manager communication in more detail.

Effective sponsor and project manager communication is vital to project success. This is not efficiently accomplished through hours of standing meetings and dozens of phone calls, email exchanges, slide shows, memoranda, and status reports each month. Sponsor communication must have a solid foundation and be adaptable to specialized needs and issues as they arise. In our experience, the sponsor and project manager should meet formally one-on-one at least monthly to review project status, risks, issues, and changes, and more frequently if project circumstances demand. The sponsor should also attend core team and steering meetings.

The goal of the Communication Package is to serve as a consolidated foundation for project status that meets the majority of the sponsor's and other stakeholders' information needs with a single resource. Imagine a Communication Package that is created at the start of a project and accumulates project history as time passes. Current project status is readily available at the front of the package, whereas detailed project history accumulates in the balance of the document.

Our example Communication Package template (Figure 4.2) begins with a cover page containing a milestone status dashboard and a notification of whether the schedule is impacted and its effect on the completion of the project. The cover is followed by the risk register, displaying high-priority active risks and their corresponding response plans. Next is the current change control log, followed by a high-level road map of the project showing inputs and expected deliverables, a statement of work, and then a key contact list for core project team members and essential stakeholders. Each section is intended to be one or two pages, primarily visual dashboards, written at an executive summary level. This design provides ready access to key information to keep senior management, core team members, and project stakeholders apprised of project status. Communication Package content is owned by the project manager who is responsible for regular maintenance throughout the life of the project.

Figure 4.2 Communication Package components

Before establishing a specific design for the Communication Package as a standard, socialize it by creating and reviewing a draft of the proposed package with the senior management team for feedback and adjust the package accordingly. When introducing the template, explain the advantages of having a project communication standard. Some key reasons include:

1. Provide a consistent mechanism for communicating project status, changes to plans, and associated risks to multiple stakeholders without creating multiple communication vehicles to deliver similar information.
2. Minimize the administrative burden on the project manager by reducing the number of communication methods and formats.
3. Provide a uniform message format that allows any reader to know where to find information they seek.

In practice the Communication Package is extremely valuable to sponsors, project managers, and stakeholders in terms of both efficiency and effectiveness. Project messaging is more consistent because stakeholders have access to the most current information. Rather than spending hours each week creating similar data for different constituencies, most communication needs can be fulfilled with a monthly or biweekly update to the Communication Package. The package can be sent to stakeholders prior to key meetings and stored in a secured and shared repository for access at any time by stakeholders who need current information. Consistency means executive sponsors can expect the same type of information in the same format on each project they sponsor, making it easier to spot areas needing focused attention. Getting information from a single consistent source rather than digging through numerous status documents and email threads allows a sponsor to make informed decisions more quickly. Comments we have received from senior managers using a similar Communication Package can be found in the accompanying text box.

> **CEO**—Give me a status vehicle that does not require me to wade through different types of documents to find out how we are doing on key projects. **CIO**—I really like this, when I receive these packages I immediately go to the risk section to determine if we have thought through the best possible risk response plan. **Sales Executive**—I love being able to stay current on each of our key project initiatives. **Executive Sponsor 1**—This is great! I use this package when discussing status or issues with the client. **Executive Sponsor 2**—Having everything in one place and in the same order makes it easy to stay current on the multiple projects I am sponsoring.

Meeting Minute Package

The Meeting Minute Package, like the Communication Package, is a standardized format that accumulates project history throughout the project's life (Figure 4.3). The package consists of a cover page with standardized meeting agenda format that covers project status, risks, major changes to the project, and then any special agenda items for a particular meeting.

PROJECT < *Insert Name of Project*>
MEETING MINUTE PACKAGE

<Insert Meeting Date>

Time: 8:30 a.m. PST / 10:30 a.m. CST / 11:30 a.m. EST
Location: (Room and/or call-in number)
Attendees: Project Team & Guests
Purpose of Meeting: To review project status
and discuss action item list.
Discussion Leader: (Project Manager Name)

Propose
DI – Discussion
DE – Decision
IS – Information Sharing

Time (mins.)	Agenda Item	Purpose	Discussion Leader	Desired Outcome
	Review Agenda	IS	PM	Agenda understood.
	Project Milestone Status	IS/DI	PM/Sponsor	Team understands current status of project
	Project Risks	IS/DI	PM	Team understands project importance.
	Project Changes	IS/DI	PM	Team understands roles and responsibilities and expectations.
	Action Items	IS/DI	PM	Issues identified and documented.
	<Special agenda topic>	TBD	TBD	TBD
	Summary	DI	PM	Questions answered.
	Close	IS	PM	Next steps identified and team understands how the meeting minutes will be reported.

OPEN - ISSUE LOG

#	Date of Issue	Priority (H/M/L)	Action	Owner	Target Date/ Resolution	Date Resolved

Figure 4.3 Meeting Minute Package template

HISTORY LOG– Listed in reverse chronological order

Date	Meeting Decisions/Notes
Xx/xx/xx	• \<Insert meeting notes • \<Insert meeting notes • Etc.
Xx/xx/xx	• \<Insert meeting notes • \<Insert meeting notes • Etc.

CLOSED – ISSUE LOG

#	Date of Issue	Priority (H/M/L)	Action	Owner	Target Date/ Resolution	Date Resolved

Figure 4.3 Meeting Minute Package template (Continued)

Following the agenda is the open issues log followed by a bullet list summary of the last meeting notes. The remainder of the Meeting Minute Package contains meeting minute summaries of all previous meetings listed in reverse chronological order, from the most recent meeting to the first project meeting. The complete historical issue log is the last section of the document.

This design has several advantages:

- The standard meeting agenda encourages all projects to cover three key areas first in every meeting, the status, any risks, and changes. This ensures that the core project team is current on each of these areas and has a shared context before covering other agenda items.
- Keeping all issues and their resolution in one package, with currently open issues upfront and closed/resolved issues at the back, helps core team members locate desired information quickly.
- The entire document serves as a project history. Sequencing the most current meetings' notes first, followed by previous meetings, allows team members to glance at the first few pages to become current and also allows a quick review of recent history to observe trends. This sequence also allows

the project manager to distribute an extract of the first pages of the document before a meeting rather than the entire document. If a core team member needs additional history, the full document can be retrieved from the repository where it is stored with other project artifacts.

- Combined with the Communication Package, the Meeting Minute Package is a valuable resource to orient a new project team member to the project and its history. If a sponsor changes midway through a project, reviewing these two documents with the project manager not only gives the incoming sponsor current information but provides a context of project events since inception.

Risk Management Process

Managing project risk is one of the project manager's most important responsibilities. Risks are uncertainties that could jeopardize project progress and success. Managing risk entails timely and active risk identification, analysis, prioritization, and development of viable options for reducing threats to the project.[5] A common tool used by the project manager, project team, and sponsor to manage risk is a risk register.

Risk Register Contents

The risk register is an accumulation of information about identified project risks. It serves as a communication device, historical journal, and tool to manage risk information. The following data are commonly recorded in the risk register for each risk:

- Risk ID—A unique identifier for each risk
- Risk Statement—A short description of the risk for reference that explains the consequences if the risk occurs
- Risk Priority—An assessment of risk significance derived from risk probability and impact

- Risk Probability—An assessment of risk likelihood
- Risk Impact—An assessment of the impact of the risk to the project and organization should it occur
- Risk Response Plan—High-level description of efforts to reduce the probability or impact of a risk as well as any contingency plans developed to address the risk or its consequences, including any changes to risk response plan for historical purposes
- Intended Resolution Date—The date the risk is believed to no longer be a risk. The risk either occurred and the risk plan implemented or the risk did not occur.
- Date Resolved—The date the risk can be marked resolved and moved to the completed section of the risk register determines no longer a threat or an opportunity.

Sponsor engagement in the risk process is critical to project success because a sponsor's strategic perspective is an essential input to the process and sponsor political power and organizational connections are often necessary for removing obstacles and securing needed resources.[6] The primary role of the sponsor in the risk management process is to approve risk response plans for high-priority risks. Only the sponsor can decide which significant risks are acceptable and when proposed mitigation strategies are sufficient. A standardized risk management process must take a system view of risk management roles. On the left are the key participants in the process. The process blocks with words represent the activities that the corresponding participant is responsible for performing. The blank process blocks represent inputs or outputs from corresponding participants depending on the direction of the arrow. If no process block is in the swim lane, then the participant does not have a role or responsibility for that step of the process. Figure 4.4 depicts a sample risk process flow using swim lanes to demonstrate responsibilities.

Writing a clear risk statement is critical to understanding a particular risk and developing proper responses. The key to effective risk statements is gaining agreement on a standardized format for capturing risks and teaching project managers and team members to write risk statements in a meaningful way. A format that we have found useful is as follows.

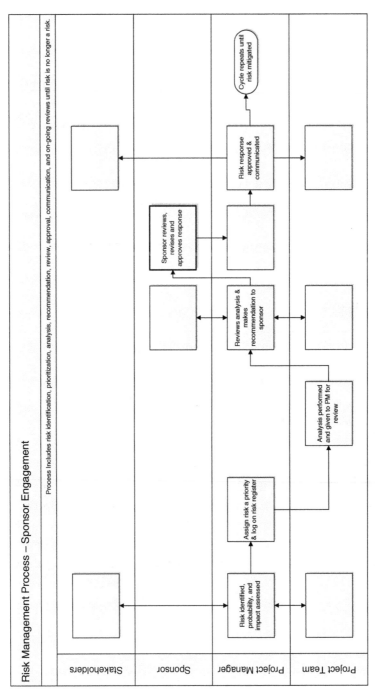

Figure 4.4 Sponsor engagement in risk management process

Format for Writing a Risk Statement

If <event that may occur> then <possible consequence to the project>.

Concisely stating what the risk event is and what the consequences could be if the risk event occurs helps the team crafting response plans focus on possible actions they could take to:

- Reduce the likelihood of a risk event occurring
- Reduce or manage the harm to the project that the event might cause
- Establish early warning systems for the risk event to maximize response time

For Example:

Example of a Risk Statement

"If <our supplier cannot provide the part by September 1> then <we will not have a functional prototype to demonstrate at the trade show September 15>".

By writing the risk statement in this format, the project team is better able to understand the situation and ramifications to the project and craft appropriate response plans. The sponsor's role is to understand the risks, their consequences to the project, and determine if the risk plans generated represent acceptable alternatives for reducing or addressing the threats. In our experience, engaging the sponsor in risk response plan review and approval has proven to be efficient and effective in helping teams to be better prepared to manage project risk and implement risk response plans should the need arise.

Change Control Process

Like risk management, project change control requires sponsor involvement to ensure changes are conscious business decisions made from a strategic perspective. All projects are subject to change pressures as they progress. Changes may come from within the project as a result of estimation errors, staff changes, incorrect assumptions, or discoveries of new or evolving requirements or opportunities. Changes may also originate outside of the project, because of changes in an organization's strategic direction, shifts in markets, suppliers, economic pressures, competitors, new regulations, or a host of other sources. Changes in project scope definition, constraints, resources, approach, or schedule can change the value proposition and risk profile of a project. The project manager's role in change management is to assure that proposed changes are thoroughly analyzed to understand overall consequences to the project's schedule, scope, resource, and other goals. The sponsor's role is to ensure that proposed changes are considered in a strategic context and do not undermine a project's value proposition. For example, a customer may ask to add new features to a product being built for them. Although customer satisfaction is important, the request must be considered in terms of the resources and time required to develop the new feature, the cost of supporting the new feature once it is delivered, any risks to project success that might be introduced by developing the new feature, and the bottom-line business case of whether the new feature positively affects the project value. All changes, even reductions of scope, increase project costs to the extent that they require replanning and modifications to the project approach, even though there might also be offsetting savings.

All Change Costs

Imagine a project to implement a new phone system in a building. The project is estimated to cost US $100k for 500 phone units, wiring, and computers. Half way through implementation, a request is made to reduce the number of phone units to 400. Casual onlookers might assume that a 20 percent reduction in the number of units would result in a corresponding cost savings. If the wiring schematics have already been approved, they will now have to be reworked at additional cost. If the wiring is already installed, there might be no cost savings for the wiring. Depending upon how the vendor prices the phone units, the reduction in the number of instruments may increase costs by

> changing volume pricing. If the units have already been delivered and are awaiting installation, the phone vendor may charge a restocking fee to return the un-needed units (or may not take them back at all). If the units have already been installed, it may actually be more expensive to deinstall them and return them than to keep them.

The change control process helps the project team assess a proposed change's impact to scope, schedule, and cost and present analysis and alternatives for sponsor selection. The sponsor can then review the alternatives and strategize with the project manager and possibly other executives on the best choices for the project and the organization. When projects are being done for external clients, the sponsor and project manager may need to strategize about who should present approved options to the customer. In any event, the sponsor must decide whether or not to make the change and accept the corresponding impacts to the project. Figure 4.5 depicts a simplified change management process that includes interaction among multiple stakeholders and their roles and responsibilities.

Processes/Tools and Sponsor Engagement

Clearly communicating the points and purpose of sponsor engagement in each of the five processes/tools described above is essential to the success of a project as well as a sponsorship initiative. The sponsor provides the senior management perspective that the project team needs. When appropriate, the sponsor can reach across organizational boundaries for necessary resources more easily because of their positional power.[7] Executive status provides sponsors more influence when negotiating both externally and internally. The Communication Package and Meeting Minute Package facilitate keeping the sponsor and other stakeholders informed of project status, whereas the standard project management life cycle, risk management, and change control processes keep the sponsor engaged in activities vital to project success. Using these processes and tools, the sponsor is positioned to influence the success of the project and provide support to the project team. Together, these help assure that key project decisions are well informed and made at the correct level of the organization.

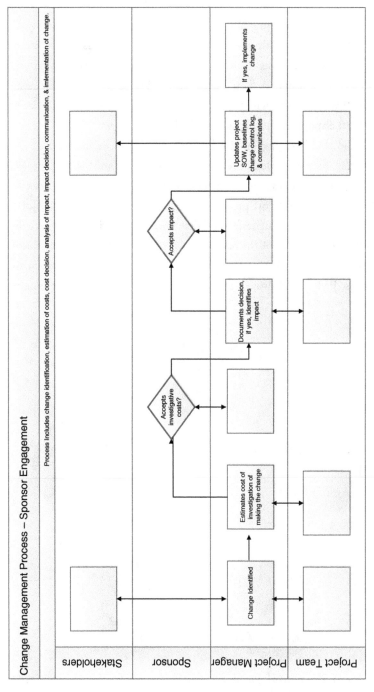

Figure 4.5 Sponsor engagement in change management process

Assess and Identify Gaps

Figure 4.6 highlights Step 2 of the framework for assessing the overall health of the sponsorship program. The cultural readiness assessment of Chapter 3 provided insight into whether an organization is ready to support project sponsorship. Step 2 uses Table 4.2 to collect data for an evaluation of whether adequate project management standards are in place to support the sponsorship role as described below.

While standardizing on the five processes/tools highlighted in this chapter is recommended, the first step toward standardizing project management practices is to determine what processes and tools are currently in place to support project management and sponsorship efforts. Look at the five tools suggested and determine what exists and where the gaps lie. This portion of the assessment could benefit greatly by gaining insight from the PMO or project managers. A task force of executive sponsors, PMO, and project managers can evaluate the current state of

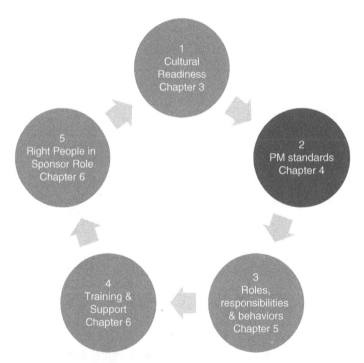

Figure 4.6 Framework for assessing a sponsorship program—project management standards focus

Table 4.2 Assessment tool—standardized processes for sponsor involvement worksheet

Best Practice Process Standards	What exists today	Compared to best practices Weak Strong 1 ← → 5				
Project Life Cycle Processes		1	2	3	4	5
Communication Package		1	2	3	4	5
Meeting Minute Package		1	2	3	4	5
Risk management process		1	2	3	4	5
Change management process		1	2	3	4	5
Etc. . . .						

project management practices using Table 4.2 to record the findings in the "What Exists" column. Then the task force can compare current practices to the best practices shared in this chapter or some other preferred standard and record a consensus score in Table 4.2 on a scale from weak to strong, using a five-point Likert scale. Once Table 4.2's assessment is complete, engage senior management in review and discussion as to the health of the current project management standards for sponsors, and then ask senior management for their overall assessment on the organization's project management standards—completing another spoke in the Organizational Preparedness spider diagram in Chapter 7—Figure 7.1.

Discussion Questions

1. What benefits do standardized project management practices offer an organization?

2. When establishing a set of standardized project management practices, why is it important to take a systems approach to design and implementation and consider the change implications that may be involved?

3. Why should project management practices be built in consultation with stakeholders?

4. If few project management practices are in place, why is it important to keep early design simple?

5. What are the advantages of having a communication standard that serves multiple audiences?

6. What are the advantages of having a Meeting Minute Package that tracks the history of the entire project life cycle?

7. Explain the sponsor role in the risk and change management processes?

Considerations

Project Management Office

If an organization's PMO serves the role of creator and keeper of project management standards, then the PMO can be of tremendous value in the assessment of the current state of project management practices. The PMO staff can identify gaps and may also be able to identify process improvements that have been proven on existing projects because of their experience across a breath of projects. Engage the PMO to leverage its knowledge of gaps but also to help orient PMO staff regarding senior management's thoughts about processes and work products. This enables the PMO to better represent those interests during implementation and provide future assistance when improvements are identified. From the PMO perspective, this is an opportunity to participate in the strategic direction of the organization by helping shape project management standards and define sponsor interactions.

The PMO is also well positioned to help prioritize and socialize implementation of new or revised standards by assuring sufficient training, documentation, and support are available when new standards are rolled out.

Project Manager

Project managers are an excellent resource for contributing to the assessment of existing standards. Project managers know where communication challenges have occurred in the past and where existing change and risk management processes are weak or nonexistent. Participation in a standard's assessment task force also provides the project managers an opportunity to collaborate with sponsors and build their leadership and negotiation skills. Project Managers will find this task force assignment an opportunity for skill growth and relationship building.

Project managers become the flag bearers for new standards when they are adopted. Teams will often take their lead from project manager behavior. If project managers embrace and work with the new standards, prepared to explain why the standards were implemented and doing so without complaint, teams are more likely to accept the cultural changes the new standards bring. If project managers fail to embrace the new standards or undermine them with complaints and begrudging compliance, team members will likely adopt a posture hostile to the new processes and make long-term adoption much more challenging.

Notes

1. Project Management Institute. 2015b. *PMI's Pulse of the Profession: Capturing the Value of Project Management,* (Newtown Square, PA: Author), p. 12.
2. Peter Senge. 1990. *The Fifth Discipline: The Art & Practice of The Learning Organization,* (New York, NY: Doubleday).
3. Project Management Institute. 2013. *A Guide to the Project Management Body of Knowledge, (PMBOK® guide)* (5th ed.), (Newtown Square, PA: Author).
4. Timothy Kloppenborg, Debbie Tesch, and Chris Manolis. 2011. "Investigation of the Sponsor's Role in Project Planning." *Management Research Review, 34*(4), 400–416. Doi:101108/01409171111117852
5. Project Management Institute, 2013, p. 309.
6. Aubry and Hobbs, 2011; Hall, Holt, and Purchase, 2003; Helm and Remington, 2005; Kloppenborg, 2012; Pinto, 2000; and Sense and Tighe, 1998.
7. Helm and Remington, 2005. "Effective Project Sponsorship: An Evaluation of the Role of the Executive Sponsor in Complex Infrastructure Projects by Senior Project Managers." *Project Management Journal, 36*(3), 51–61.

CHAPTER 5

Desirable Executive Sponsor Characteristics

"Effective sponsorship is largely dependent upon the personal characteristics and behavior of the individuals carrying out the role."[1]

Desirable executive sponsor characteristics are the roles, responsibilities, and behaviors recommended for consideration when crafting or enhancing the sponsor role. This chapter explores current thinking for baselining these areas and provides insight into why effectively executing these characteristics positively influences project outcomes. Behaviors and temperaments are discussed first to lay a foundation as to why just having clear roles and responsibilities are not enough. The combination of all of these characteristics is necessary to effectively execute the executive sponsor role.

Desirable Behaviors and Temperaments

Project sponsors do not have to be perfect but they need to be willing to adapt their style to the project context to be effective.[2] Beyond sponsor roles and responsibilities, in this chapter we also explore behaviors and temperaments necessary for effective executive sponsorship, and use scenarios to provide examples and rationale for our assertions. Figure 5.1 highlights the behaviors and temperaments to be explored.

Academic research and our experience agree that three key project sponsor behaviors are directly associated with performance.[3]

- Excellent communication and listening skills
- Artful handling of ambiguity
- Ability to manage self

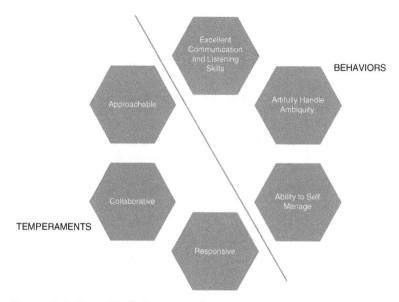

Figure 5.1 Desirable behaviors and temperaments

When one or more of these behaviors is deficient, the project sponsor's effectiveness is diminished and the project manager must then try to compensate and deal with the additional risks introduced by the sponsor. Dealing with sponsor shortcomings increases project chaos and increases the project manager's workload, taking time away from other project management activities. In the following sections we explore these sponsor behaviors and temperaments and why they are important.

Communication and Listening Skills

Sponsors need to communicate effectively with everyone who influences the project. This could be their peers, the client, the project manager, the project team, and various stakeholders such as partners, vendors, or other interested parties. As examples, sponsors brief the executive team, justify continued project investment, and provide direction and counsel to the project manager. In addition, they make decisions on scope, schedule, or cost changes and evaluate the merits of risk-response plans. Each of these responsibilities requires effective communication skill for understanding, influencing, negotiating, motivating, and empathizing with various constituencies.

To communicate effectively, sponsors need to be active listeners. Active listening describes the active process of giving the person speaking your full attention and confirming your understanding of what has been said before responding. It is a skill that can be learned, but it takes practice and effort. The ability to listen is critical when trying to expose a problem, understand the concerns of others, or determine and prioritize action. Whether exploring the basis of disagreements, searching for compromise, or responding to a crisis or new information, sponsors need to determine when to lead and when to mentor. They do this by actively listening to their team[4] and stakeholders. Active listening is also a powerful motivation tool. Being an engaged listener improves morale and helps build and sustain relationships.[5] When project team members feel someone is listening they are more likely to believe they have a voice and their opinions are welcomed and heard. This is not only good for the team, but it also encourages timely delivery of bad news as well as discussion of unpopular or controversial opinions or information that might otherwise be lost.

Effective Communication

When conducting project reviews of failed projects it is common for leadership to claim that it was blind-sided by the failure and that there was little or no warning from the project team. Conversations with team members often paint a significantly different picture. Teams often report being aware that projects were in trouble or beyond hope months before the failure was apparent. When asked why this information was not shared with leadership, the three most common answers we have encountered are:

1. We tried to tell our leaders, but they did not listen
2. Leadership made clear that they did not want to know about problems
3. We were told to "stop being so negative"

Artful Handling of Ambiguity

The second key behavior is the art of handling ambiguity, and it is one of the major challenges facing sponsors especially in complex programs and projects.[6] Complex projects constantly change and evolve and sponsors must give clear direction and make rapid decisions to keep the effort on track. Making decisions in the face of uncertainty requires courage and wisdom; the courage to be wrong, and the wisdom to know when to act and when to wait for more information. When problems or conflicting priorities emerge, the project manager looks to the sponsor for direction to choose among available options for the best response.

Handling Ambiguity

Conventional management wisdom suggests leaders gather all relevant facts before making a decision, sometimes unintentionally stalling decisions to the detriment of the project. Effective sponsors add notable qualifiers to the competencies of decisiveness and responsiveness, respectively, making "clear and responsible" decisions and "rapid and thoughtful" responses. Sponsor should consider the following as part of all decision making:

1. Is this issue time sensitive?
2. What are the risks and costs of a delayed decision?
3. Are there plausible solutions available?
4. Are there adequate facts to make a decision?
5. What are the pros and cons of this decision?
6. Is there an acceptable and defendable explanation and rationale for decision?

Sponsors who adapt to change, make timely crucial decisions, and offer clear direction in times of uncertainty are perceived as more competent leaders. Their decisive actions allow the project team to sustain forward momentum, adjust plans, and execute. On the other hand, late decisions and poor decisions are detrimental to project success and team morale. Responsiveness and decisiveness are valued. Sponsors should not make their teams work harder or wait longer than necessary to get a decision.

Desirable sponsor leadership characteristics for dealing with ambiguity:

- Seek to understand the issues and consider all available information.
- Solicit and assess the opinions of others and engage team members in the decision-making process when appropriate.
- Look for unstated assumptions that may be influencing recommendations.
- Make tough decisions promptly.
- Explain the rationale for decisions—this enables project managers to anticipate sponsor thinking and refine the information and options presented in the future.
- Be clear when giving direction.
- Keep stakeholders apprised of decisions.
- When a previous decision must be changed, use facts and explain why.
- When mistakes are discovered, own them and deal with the consequences.

Ability to Manage Self

The third key sponsor behavior is the ability to manage self. Executive sponsorship cannot become one of many "other duties as assigned." The sponsors are accountable for managing their time and priorities. Although sponsorship is typically not an executive's only duty, sponsors must be capable of balancing competing demands for their time and attention and assuring the project receives an appropriate share.[7]

When project challenges arise, project manager's access to the sponsor is essential. The frequency of interaction necessary between project manager and sponsor can vary over the life of the project.[8] It is important to understand the project management process and sponsor roles and responsibilities at each stage of the project to anticipate the level of support a project manager requires as a project progresses. This can be complicated when working with project managers of different experience levels. Project managers have strengths and weaknesses just like sponsors, and some need more sponsor guidance than others. Complex projects generally require a greater commitment of sponsor time. No matter the complexity, projects encountering trouble require more sponsor time.

Managing Self

Demonstrating the ability to manage self is not only important with respect to correctly allocating sponsor time and attention; it demonstrates commitment to the project and models effective behavior for the project manager and the team.

Self-management can be demonstrated in a number of ways:

- Arriving promptly for scheduled meetings
- Not allowing sponsor participation in team events to be disrupted for anything other than true emergencies (ignoring cell phones, discouraging others from interrupting meetings for calls or signatures)
- When accepting a task, ensuring follow-through
- Respecting commitments made to the project team for decisions or turnaround of document reviews

Being Responsive, Collaborative, and Approachable

The findings regarding communication, ambiguity, and self-management are consistent with our experience, although we would add/emphasize that being responsive, collaborative, and approachable are essential traits as well. Keeping in mind that projects are temporary endeavors,[9] choosing to display these temperaments aids the sponsor in creating an environment that energizes the team.

For example:

- Promptly responding to meeting requests
- Promptly responding to email or voice mail
- Taking the time to thoughtfully answer questions
- Giving credit to others for their good ideas
- Seeking opportunities for informal conversations with the project manager over breakfast, coffee, or lunch
- Welcoming and seeking the input of others
- Explicitly acknowledging mistakes
- When decisions or guidance change, discussing the change and explaining the rationale behind it

Exploring Current Roles and Responsibilities

Describing and encouraging desired sponsor behavior establishes goals, but does not provide actionable information about current sponsor performance and how to achieve improvement. Sponsors must consistently exhibit these behaviors in the context of performing their role and responsibilities to be effective. How might sponsor performance be gauged? Self-assessment is relatively easy, but has limitations. Research shows that sponsors typically rate themselves higher than project teams in the performance of their role.[10] As outlined in Chapter 1, there are tools available to frame and assess the necessary competencies for sponsorship, such as the Global Alliance for Project Performance Standards (GAPPS) Framework. Recognizing that there are different approaches for implementing project sponsorship and judging performance, GAPPS' "Guiding Framework for Project Sponsors" provides one performance-based method for assessing sponsor roles and responsibilities. The primary roles that comprise sponsorship in the GAPPS framework are[11]:

1. Taking accountability for the project—Accountability means that the sponsor is responsible for how well the project is managed, the success or failure of the product or service the project provides, and the realization of benefits to be achieved by the project.
2. Supporting the project manager—The project manager has day-to-day responsibility for the project, whereas the sponsor has overall responsibility for the outcomes. Support in this context refers to being available to the project manager for questions and guidance, providing timely information regarding project and organizational priorities, and facilitating resolution of organizational and political issues beyond the authority of the project manager. It also includes providing the project manager with feedback on his or her performance.
3. Supporting the project—This includes providing resources, decision making, cultivating and sustaining stakeholder commitment, and participating in project reviews.

A table outlining the GAPPS Sponsorship Framework appears below. For purposes of relating GAPPS material to the terminology in our book, "Units" represent sponsor roles, "Elements" are examples and aspects of the associated responsibilities for each role, and "Performance Criteria" are measurable and observable ways to assess how well the role and responsibility are being executed:

The GAPPS framework is a tool used to assess an individual sponsor based on his or her observed performance to determine that individual's likelihood of being able to perform the role competently in the future, while providing feedback about opportunities for improvement and professional development. This assessment assumes a sponsor is considered competent only if he or she satisfies 100 percent of the performance criteria through the evidence supplied in a dialogue with the assessor. If all performance criteria are not met, the sponsor would be assessed "unable to provide evidence of competency" in that area.[12] The assessment results could be useful input to a development plan.

Although the framework is thorough and helpful for assessing roles and responsibilities, a bit more context may help clarify why these sponsorship behaviors and temperaments are such important aspects of executive sponsorship. Scenarios are presented below that examine each of the roles and its associated responsibilities in Table 5.1.

Role 1. Take Accountability for the Project

Projects are undertaken because the business outcome to be delivered is believed valuable to the organization. Although the value proposition may be complex and involve many parts of the organization, the sponsor is the keeper and chief arbiter of that value. Although it is reasonable to expect a project manager to attend to a project's business case, the sponsor has primary responsibility for assuring that the initial business case is sound. Monitoring emerging information about the business context, the organization's goals and direction, and the project itself as the effort progresses to assure all remain aligned is the sponsor's responsibility.

The following three scenarios provide context for evaluating a sponsor's ability to "take accountability for the project" while demonstrating effective behaviors. Each scenario could also serve as a situational training tool for sponsor professional development.

Scenario: The Orphan

In your new role as executive sponsor you inherit a project to develop and implement a new automated time keeping process throughout the

Table 5.1 Summary of roles, responsibilities, and performance criteria worksheet[13]

Roles	Responsibilities	
Units	**Elements**	**Performance Criteria**
1. Take accountability for the project	1.1 Ensure the project is justified	1.1.1 Alignment of the project with the defined direction of the organization is maintained.
		1.1.2 The project is justified and realistic.
	1.2 Sustain effective governance.	1.2.1 Authority levels, approval process, decision making protocols, and reporting mechanisms are defined, communicated, and implemented.
		1.2.2 Project governance complies with applicable requirements.
		1.2.3 Socially responsible practice is actively supported.
		1.2.4 Sponsorship role is clearly defined and communicated to relevant stakeholders.
		1.2.5 Lessons learned process is supported.
		1.2.6 Ownership of the product of the project is transferred.
	1.3 Orchestrate plans for benefits realisation.	1.3.1 The path to benefits realisation is clearly defined, feasible and communicated.
		1.3.2 Ownership of benefits realisation is identified, understood, and accepted by the relevant stakeholders.
2. Support the project manager	2.1 Be available to the project manager.	2.1.1 Commitments to the project manager are planned and kept.
		2.1.2 Relevant information is shared with the project manager in a timely manner.
		2.1.3 Project manager's requests are addressed in a timely manner.
	2.2 Assist the project manager with conflict management.	2.2.1 Potential conflicts are anticipated and managed.
		2.2.2 Conflicts beyond the capacity of the project manager are dealt with in a timely manner.
		2.2.3 Project manager's role in dealing with conflict is reinforced.
	2.3 Provide feedback on the performance of the project manager.	2.3.1 Performance of the project manager is assessed.
		2.3.2 Actions are taken to ensure that the project manager applies good practice.

(Continued)

Table 5.1 Summary of roles, responsibilities, and performance criteria worksheet[13]

Roles	Responsibilities	
Units	Elements	Performance Criteria
3. Support the project	3.1 Resource availability is sustained.	3.1.1 Project and organisation resource needs are addressed.
		3.1.2 Funding approval is secured.
		3.1.3 Project context is monitored and evaluated for circumstances that may affect resource readiness.
		3.1.4 Action is take to resolve resource issues.
	3.2 Cultivate Stakeholder commitments.	3.2.1 Personal commitment to the sponsor role is demonstrated.
		3.2.2 Approaches to sustaining stakeholder commitment are defined and supported.
		3.2.3 Visibility of the project is promoted to relevant stakeholders.
		3.2.4 Stakeholder interests and expectations are monitored.
		3.2.5 Differences in stakeholder interests and expectations are reconciled.
		3.2.6 Project achievements are recognised.
	3.3 Ensure readiness for project reviews.	3.3.1 Project reviews are planned and occur in a timely manner.
		3.3.2 Actions are taken to ensure personal readiness for project reviews.
		3.3.3. Constructive feedback on project team's preparation is provided prior to external reviews.
	3.4 Provide decisions in a timely manner.	3.4.1 Decisions are made as scheduled.
		3.4.2 Decisions that are escalated to the sponsor are resolved in a timely manner.
		3.4.3 Actions are taken to overcome impact on the project due to others delaying decisions.

enterprise and integrate it with the existing payroll system. In discussions with the project manager, you are unable to identify a business justification for the project. There is no apparent relationship between this project and the organization's strategic plan. What should the sponsor do?

GAPPS 1.1 Ensure the Project is Justified

- The value of this project should be questioned. Does it offer significant cost savings or productivity improvement? Is the system mandated? What is the problem the system seeks to solve? If the project manager is unaware of a compelling business case, it might be appropriate to reach out to other executives to determine if a business case exists now or ever existed. This project may have been started without proper vetting, or the business need may have faded after the project was launched. One of a sponsor's primary roles is to assure that any project in the portfolio is the best use of organizational resources at the present time.

- Although the sponsor is the guardian of the business case, the project manager should always be aware of the business imperative so that it can guide his or her decision making. This scenario presents a mentoring opportunity for the sponsor to reinforce the project manager's role with respect to the business case. If the project manager offered concerns about the business justification to the sponsor unbidden, this is an opportunity for the sponsor to appreciate and encourage that behavior. If the lack of business justification only emerged in response to sponsor questions, the sponsor might encourage the project manager to raise the issue if ever the business value of the project appears questionable.

- The team should also be made aware of the project business case. Team members will often see tactical opportunities to better address the business need while they are engaged in the project, provided they are clear on the project goals and priorities. Teams that understand the project rationale can bring these opportunities to the attention of leadership for consideration.

This scenario underscores the relationship between the project manager and the sponsor, and the role of the sponsor as the principle custodian of the business case. The sponsor and project manager are partners in delivering business value, but the sponsor monitors the value proposition for change. The sponsor is the first line of defense for the organization in terms of realigning the project, redefining it, or stopping it should the business case unravel.

Scenario: Noncompliance

A project review determines that your project is not following standards mandated for your regulated industry. What should the sponsor do?

GAPPS 1.2 Sustain Effective Governance

- Meet promptly with the project manager to discuss the finding. Was noncompliance a choice or an oversight? Who made this choice? What was the rationale? What are the consequences of the choice? Did the person making the decision have the authority to do so? Do project records reflect the decision? Is this a decision that should have been made by the sponsor?
- Determine whether similar decisions or omissions have been made.
- Assess this issue's effect on the business case? Is the project still valuable?

Although there should always be room for human mistakes, this scenario focuses on the challenge of assessing the difference between incompetence, sloppiness, business decisions, and honest errors. Just as the project manager establishes the ethical tone for the team, the sponsor establishes the ethical tone for the project and ensures that effective governance is sustained. Intentionally "failing to notice" a true requirement should only occur with sponsor consultation and approval.

The project manager and sponsor must develop and sustain an open dialog about project issues so that surprises like this do not occur. In this case, the sponsor should mentor the project manager while jointly analyzing the situation and deciding the next course of action. This scenario also ties closely to the sponsor's responsibility of providing feedback on the performance of the project manager.

Scenario: Riches to Rags

Your organization has had a string of successful products and is flush with cash. A project is launched to develop a new product to complement the existing product line. Comparable products exist, but marketing believes a solid, minimal-function product under your brand could be sold to existing customers. The development effort is expected to take 18 months. Six months after the project begins, there is a significant financial downturn and capital becomes tight. The portfolio of projects is reviewed for nonessential projects that can be killed or deferred. What should the sponsor do?

GAPPS 1.3 Orchestrate Plans for Benefits Realization

- An effective sponsor will keep the project manager apprised of the effects of the economic downturn on the organization and might encourage the project manager to review plans to see if there are ways to further reduce costs by extending the schedule or trimming functionality in anticipation of resource constraints.
- Although there may be insufficient information outlined in the brief scenario above to justify a decision to kill the project, the project's business case should certainly be reviewed in light of emerging economic conditions for possible termination, deferral, or trimming of scope.

This scenario underscores the nature of the relationship to be built and sustained between the sponsor and the project manager as well as the necessity of the sponsor monitoring the performance and priorities of the organization to anticipate impacts to projects. When project benefits appear to be waning it is the sponsor's responsibility to reassess business value in consultation with relevant stakeholders.

Role 2. Support the Project Manager

Support for the project manager includes helping the project manager navigate organizational politics; assuring the project manager has ready access to the sponsor to obtain decisions, guidance and assistance; providing the project manager with timely access to strategic information affecting the project; and monitoring project manager performance and providing timely feedback. The following three scenarios highlight sponsor responsibilities.

Scenario: Market Evaporates

Your organization has identified an unserved niche in the marketplace and initiated a project to fill that niche. The development effort is expected to take 12 months. Shortly after the project begins, the project manager becomes aware that a larger competitor has announced and begun to ship a more feature-rich product than your project is building, which is priced at 80 percent of your target price. The project manager meets with the sponsor and shares this new information. What should the sponsor do?

GAPPS 2.1 Be Available to the Project Manager

- Recognize the project manager for taking the initiative to contact the sponsor. Project managers and team members often incorrectly assume that executives have perfect and timely information regarding all aspects of a project's industry, marketplace, and applicable knowledge domains. A project manager who recognizes this information about a competitor is relevant and seeks out the sponsor promptly to assure it is known should be encouraged.

- Although there may be strategic reasons to continue the project, the business case should be reviewed. Perhaps project scope should be reassessed? Is the product sales and marketing group willing to price the product you are developing more competitively? Part of this conversation should occur with the project manager, and part with other significant project stakeholders.
- Relevant information obtained from other executive stakeholders that guide the project response to this situation should be shared with the project manager so that appropriate alternatives can be derived and options presented.

The project sponsor and project manager must both monitor the emerging facts as the project progresses and continually reassess the business case. This scenario again underscores the role of the sponsor as the liaison between the strategic (what are the organization's priorities and what makes business sense?) and the tactical (what must we do to accomplish this project as defined?). It can be difficult for individuals in an organization to confront changing facts about project viability. Someone in the sales organization may have pushed hard to get this project authorized, and it may have been the best decision with the information available at the time. When the facts on the ground change, the sponsor should lead a reassessment of business value.

Scenario: Unmanaged Scope

Your organization is performing a fixed-price project for an external client. The client is consistently failing to meet their obligations for providing essential information and resources to the project team and it is impacting the schedule and cost of performing the project. Your organization's sales team (key stakeholder, but not part of your project team) is hesitant to approach the client to address responsibility for client-induced schedule and cost increases. What should the sponsor do?

GAPPS 2.2 Assist the Project Manager with Conflict Management

- Review project plans and client status reports with the project manager. Are client responsibilities clearly articulated? Have previous client failures to meet obligations been documented and shared with the client? Is the change control process being appropriately utilized to request the client take responsibility for the cost and schedule implications of delays that are caused by client action or inaction?
- If the project manager is not appropriately administering the change control process then this deficiency should be corrected.
- If the sales team is interfering with appropriate project administration, this may require executive-level diplomacy to either increase the project budget [decrease project return on investment (ROI)] to accede to the wishes of the sales team, or align the sales team with the change control process. This is an example of the sponsor assisting the project manager with conflict resolution within the organization that may be beyond the project manager's political capacity.
- If the client is resistant to the change control process, it may require executive-level diplomacy to encourage the client to fulfill their obligations or seek contractual relief. This would be an example of the sponsor assisting the project manager with conflict resolution outside of the organization. The project manager likely does not have the authority to suggest project termination to a client, making the project manager a poor candidate negotiator in this circumstance.

An enterprise may make a business decision to reduce its profit margin on a project being done for a client and absorb client-initiated cost over-runs rather than enforce change control, but this should be a conscious decision made by executives with appropriate authority. Quietly allowing the client to delay the schedule or increase the budget without penalty, both fails to discourage that expensive client behavior and sets the project up to disappoint executives with its financial performance and the client with schedule performance. A sponsor may often be required to educate other parts of his or her organization (project manager, peers, and executive management) regarding the consequences of these choices. The sponsor may also need to make clear to a client organization that both the client and the service provider must uphold their obligations to deliver a quality product or service consistent with the time and costs spelled out in joint agreements. The project manager should enforce change control, but the sponsor may be required to be its ambassador. It is the sponsor's responsibility to assist the project manager with conflict management.

Scenario: Unmanaged Risk

A 30-month product development project has been underway for 10 months. During a recent status meeting, the project manager informs you that another key supplier will be unable to meet previous commitments. This is the fourth time since project's inception that one of its suppliers has been unable to meet prior commitments. What should the project sponsor do?

GAPPS 2.3 Provide Feedback on the Performance of the Project Manager

- If this were an isolated incident, you might ask the project manager for ideas about how to minimize the impact on the project. If this appears to be a trend, then there may also be a larger issue emerging. Review the project's risk management approach and plans. Have any actions been initiated to address this problem now that it has occurred several times? Were there any indications that suppliers were having trouble meeting their obligations? Were the original commitments from the supplier reasonable and entered into willingly?
- Is there evidence that project risk is being actively managed? Failure to effectively manage risk would call into question the skills and experience of the project manager.

This scenario underscores the sponsor's duty to monitor the project manager's performance. Sponsors should recognize the difference between good luck and good management as well as bad luck and bad management. Project managers experiencing bad luck should be protected from consequences for outcomes beyond their control. Project managers who are not adequately managing the project should either be remediated or replaced. The sponsor is responsible for monitoring project manager performance and addressing shortcomings.

Role 3. Support the Project

For the final role, we expand the role beyond supporting the project manager to supporting the project and facilitating overall project success. The sponsor provides organizational resources to the project manager to address the needs of the project. Sometimes these resources may be under the sponsor's control; other times they may be provided by other parts of the organization. The sponsor must assure that promised resources are provided and address resource issues when they arise. The sponsor also monitors the organizational context for changes that might affect the project. Four scenarios offer examples of the behaviors sponsors exhibit while supporting the project.

Scenario: The Impossible Dream

You take over the role of executive sponsor midway through a product development project. Early discussions with the project manager indicate she has significant concerns about the organization's ability to complete the project successfully within the allotted cost and schedule because sister organizations are not fulfilling their resource commitments. What should the sponsor do?

GAPPS 3.1 Resource Availability is Sustained

- Meet promptly with the project manager to understand her concerns. Is this an emerging issue, or has it been acknowledged previously?

- Determine what actions need to be taken to resolve resource issues. The project manager monitors the resources needed, promised, and provided. The sponsor may need to intervene if these commitments are not being kept.
- Confirm the resources that are necessary. If the current cost and schedule do not appear to be feasible, what would a more credible cost and schedule be? Are there ways to reduce scope to fit within available time and resources? What are the current project priorities? How do various recovery scenarios affect the underlying business case for the project?
- Sponsors must be prepared to act upon the best information available, either changing the project boundaries to make them attainable or canceling a project that no longer makes good business sense.

Effective sponsors must disabuse themselves of the myth that all projects are feasible. The project manager serves as the sponsor's eyes and ears, monitoring project feasibility as new information becomes available. Sponsors should recognize the difference between a project manager whining, which should be discouraged, and a project manager raising significant risks or concerns, which is a key project manager responsibility to be expected and encouraged. In this scenario, the sponsor's responsibility is ensuring an accurate understanding of the resources required, confirming that the organization is able and willing to provide those resources, and determining whether the project remains feasible.

Scenario: Stakeholder Management

Your project will be implementing a new accounting system throughout your organization. The project is being phased in to various parts of the organization over time. A steering committee has been formed consisting of executive representatives of each part of the organization. Midway through the effort, the project manager reports that one of the organization's divisions has not been meeting their schedule targets for preparation and seeks your assistance. The project manager reports that efforts to reach out to the executive representative of that division have been rebuffed repeatedly over the past 4 weeks. What should the sponsor do?

GAPPS 3.2 Cultivate Stakeholder Commitment

- An effective sponsor needs to gather information to determine if this is a project issue that should be addressed by the project manager, or a political issue that should be addressed at an executive level. First steps would be to determine the history and extent of the problem and review the project manager's efforts thus far. If there is evidence of a significant problem that has been occurring for some time, it might be appropriate mentoring to encourage the project manager to seek your assistance sooner in similar circumstances.

- Are the project manager's efforts to address the issue thus far sufficient? Are there additional actions you would expect the project manager to perform before escalating the issue to you? If the project manager's efforts seem reasonable, it may be appropriate for the sponsor to reach out to the executive to address the issue diplomatically. Does the executive and his/ her department concur with the priority of the project? Is the organization getting the support needed from the project? Should the schedule be adjusted? Problem solving at the executive level is the responsibility of the sponsor.

This scenario emphasizes the sponsor's responsibility to cultivate stakeholder commitment. Project managers are often required to seek co-operation and assistance from other parts of the organization. When promised or necessary assistance is not forthcoming, it is reasonable to expect the project manager to escalate appropriately, but there are sometimes political issues that only a sponsor can address. The sponsor's responsibility is to cultivate and sustain stakeholder commitments. If stakeholders are not honoring their commitments, the sponsor should address the situation.

Scenario: Lack of progress

The project began 6 months ago. Recent status reports indicate the project is not making progress initially expected and it is trending significantly over budget. What should the project sponsor do?

GAPPS 3.3 Ensure Readiness for Project Reviews

- Day-to-day project performance is the purview of the project manager; however, it is incumbent upon the sponsor to monitor project and project manager performance to assure that the underlying causes of schedule, scope, and resource variance are identified and addressed. The sponsor should request a briefing by the project manager of the issues that seem to be driving the schedule and resource challenges being experienced. Is the project manager's assessment credible? Does the project manager have a path forward that credibly addresses identified issues? Does the project manager need assistance? These questions might trigger a project review to get a second opinion on the viability of existing plans.
- Determine whether the project is still feasible. Were initial assumptions and estimates of cost and schedule too optimistic? Does the business case remain viable? If schedule and cost have changed significantly, it may be appropriate to reconsider the value of the project and perhaps replan with the information now available.
- Assess whether there are specific issues responsible for slowing progress or increasing costs. Are these issues that the project manager can address, or is executive action required to address them?
- Consider initiating a formal project review. It can sometimes be difficult for an organization to dispassionately assess the soundness of a project approach, the performance of a team, and the accuracy of project status. Often the members of the organization most capable of the assessment are part of

(Continued)

> the project team and may lose perspective or share unstated
> or unconscious assumptions about the project and the
> context in which it is being performed. One solution to this
> potential myopic bias is a project review performed by a team
> uninvolved in the project. Project reviews typically consist of a
> team of reviewers meeting with the project team and reviewing
> project artifacts to render an opinion about the health of the
> project and raising or emphasizing any issues that appear to be
> under-reported or underappreciated.

Projects are generally started with the best of intentions. Everyone assumes the business case is reasonable and the schedule and budget are viable. These beliefs are based upon assumptions about the project and the business context that may be optimistic or may change with time and experience. Sponsors must remain vigilant that the realities of the project are generally aligned with the initial assumptions, and prepared to act when data suggest action is warranted. In their "support the project manager" role, the sponsor seeks to understand the reasons for lack of progress before acting, while at the same time mentoring the project manager as to the types of questions they should be asking and prepared to answer. Building trust with the project manager is critical, so the project manager feels comfortable in keeping the sponsor informed regardless of what the message might be. External reviews are a way of validating both project and project manager performance and gaining an independent assessment of project status and viability.

Scenario: Client Deal Requires Accelerated Schedule

Your organization releases new versions of your software product annually to provide new features to customers and correct maintenance issues that have been identified. Six months into sponsoring the next product iteration project, sales informs you that a significant deal with a large new client is dependent upon your team delivering some of the promised new functions 3 months earlier than planned. What should the sponsor do?

GAPPS 3.4 Provide Decisions in a Timely Manner

- An effective sponsor will resist the temptation to agree to the schedule change without consulting the project manager. Although the business case may be compelling, the feasibility, cost, and risk of accelerating the schedule should be carefully assessed and considered before decisions and commitments are made.
- Confer with the project manager about the opportunity. Are there options that might address the emergent request? Can the scope of the release be reduced to meet the schedule? What are the implications to the project of spinning off a separate product to meet the special customer need? Does researching this issue now jeopardize the normal delivery schedule?
- Discuss the customer situation with sales and work with sales executives to involve the executive suite to ensure the organization is making the best decision and is aware of any necessary risks and trade-offs.

This scenario emphasizes the partnership between the project manager and the sponsor. The reconciliation of emerging business opportunities and project obligations requires the sponsor understand the business case and the project manager know the status of the project and what options might be available. Done well, this is an opportunity for joint problem solving at its finest. Any possible strategies that change the nature of existing commitments or increase project costs would likely require vetting with the executive team, but that conversation should be based on the best information available about project status and the implications of any proposed change. It is also essential that the sponsor communicate the problem-solving process and any trade-offs agreed upon to the executive team to avoid the mistaken perception, "we asked for it three months earlier and they gave it to us without any increased cost, loss of functionality, or increased risk." Few changes of this nature are "free" and the sponsor is the best person on the executive team to promote this fact.

Assessing Executive Sponsorship Characteristics

Figure 5.2 illustrates the third step in the assessment of the organization's readiness to implement or enhance a sponsorship program. The material in this chapter should help determine whether sponsor roles, responsibilities, and behaviors currently in place are adequate for the organization.

The first step in the assessment of the sponsorship characteristics is to review current sponsor roles and responsibilities. Using the GAPPS criteria in Table 5.1, color-code or shade the roles, responsibilities, and performance criteria that most closely emulate sponsor standards used within the organization. The resulting modified GAPPS chart provides a holistic view when determining gaps, making it easier to see possible voids. To fill the gaps, add, delete, or modify roles, responsibilities, and performance criteria to fit organizational needs.

The current state of sponsorship behaviors and temperaments in the organization can be assessed in two different ways using Table 5.2.

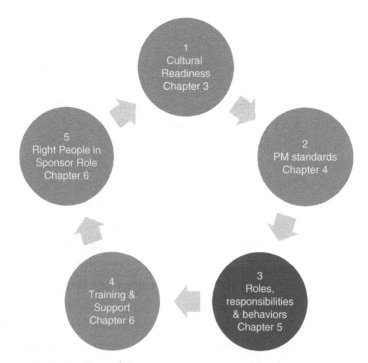

Figure 5.2 Framework for assessing a sponsorship program—focus on roles, responsibilities, and behaviors

Table 5.2 Assessment worksheet for desired behavior and temperaments

Desired behaviors and temperaments	Current expected behavior and temperaments Weak 1 ← → 5 Strong					Gaps
Excellent communication and listening skills	1	2	3	4	5	
Artfully handle ambiguity	1	2	3	4	5	
Ability to self-manage	1	2	3	4	5	
Responsiveness	1	2	3	4	5	
Collaboration	1	2	3	4	5	
Approachable	1	2	3	4	5	

1. If an organization currently recognizes the sponsor role, project managers, sponsors, and Project Management Office (PMO) leaders might use the table as a survey regarding observed sponsor behaviors on projects that were active during the past year, completed or not. The scores for each of the indicated characteristics could be averaged and considered the "current state" of sponsorship in the organization. A resulting score is not intended to be statistically valid but rather an indication to promote further discussion.

2. Organizations that are new to sponsorship and have no significant track record might ask the executive team to anonymously score three of their peers using the characteristics of Table 5.2 and then use the average of those scores for the entire team to establish a baseline of the current state of sponsorship in the organization.

Either method will generate a starting point for the training and skills development conversation that will be explored in Chapter 6.

Once perceptions about the current state and gaps are recorded in Tables 5.1 and 5.2, use these data to engage senior management in discussion for determining the health of sponsor roles, responsibilities, and behaviors. Following the discussion, have senior management assess and record their consensus on the organization's Roles, Responsibilities, and Behaviors element of the spider diagram in Figure 7.1. This score will provide a baseline for improvements, which is discussed in Chapter 8.

Discussion Questions

1. Why are personal characteristics and behaviors of the person in the sponsor role important?

2. Identify six desired sponsor behaviors and explain why each is important to project success. For each of these behaviors, rate a sponsor you have interacted with from 0 to 2 on his or her performance (0 = Does not do this, 1 = Does this sometimes, 2 = Does this consistently).

3. How might weaknesses in one area counteract strengths in another?

4. Why is sponsorship assessment essential?

5. What approaches or tools might be used for assessment? What are the advantages and disadvantages of these approaches or tools?

6. What aspects of effective sponsorship can be taught and how?

7. What aspects of effective sponsorship cannot be taught? Why?

Considerations

Project Management Office

The PMO is in an excellent position to document the current roles, responsibilities, and behaviors of executive sponsors. Use this opportunity to share what standards exist and showcase good practices not used consistently by all sponsors.

Project Manager

Project managers are also an excellent position to share best practices that have contributed to project success as well as identify areas where sponsorship assistance could be improved. Leverage this knowledge pool and tap project managers to provide input.

The ability to provide input safely, without fear of punishment or criticism, is key. Project managers' input helps shape sponsor roles, responsibilities, and behaviors that are critical to project success.

Notes

1. Lynn Crawford, Terry Cooke-Davies, Brian Hobbs, Les Labuscha-gne, Kaye Remington, and Ping Chen. 2008b. *Situational Sponsorship of Project and Programs,* (Newtown Square, PA: Project Management Institute), p. xi.
2. Vicki James, Ron Rosenhead, and Peter Taylor. 2013. *Strategies for Project Sponsorship,* (Tysons Corner, VA: Management Concepts), p. 73.
3. Crawford et al. 2008b, p. 75.
4. Timothy J. Kloppenborg and Lawrence J. Laning.. 2012. *Strategic Leadership of Portfolio and Project Management,* (New York, NY: Business Expert Press), p. 59.
5. Crawford et al. 2008b, p. 69.
6. Crawford et al. 2008b, pp. 47–50 and 69–70.
7. Crawford et al. 2008b, p. 71.
8. Kloppenborg and Laning, 2012, p. 47.
9. Project Management Institute. 2013. *A guide to the project management body of knowledge, (PMBOK® guide)* (5th ed.), (Newtown Square, PA: Author), p. 553.
10. Crawford et al. 2008b.
11. GAPPS, 2015, p. 7.
12. Ibid.
13. GAPPS, 2015, p.4.

CHAPTER 6

Sponsor Readiness

"...'Would you tell me, please, which way I ought to go from here?'
'That depends a good deal on where you want to get to,' said the Cat.
'I don't much care where –' said Alice.
'Then it doesn't matter which way you go,' said the Cat."
—Lewis Carroll,
Alice's Adventures in Wonderland[1]

We believe effective sponsors are made, not born—so the question arises, "How can an organization select and groom competent, but possibly inexperienced executives to prepare them for the sponsor role?" Thus far, we have suggested a high standard for project sponsor performance, but not addressed how sponsors might acquire the skills and tools needed to be effective. Learning on the job can be costly and painful and it is unrealistic to assume that sponsors will naturally gain the requisite skills on their path to the executive suite. Though a few executives may rise from the ranks of project performance and project management, many may have excelled instead at leadership, finance, sales, marketing, or operations and have little practical project management experience. In Chapter 2, we discussed why executive sponsorship matters and highlighted examples of how sponsorship provides an opportunity for both personal growth and professional development. This chapter emphasizes the importance of assessing executive readiness for the sponsor role and suggests ways for senior management to evaluate and cultivate effective sponsors by providing training and mentoring to address gaps.

Not everyone is well suited for sponsorship. If an individual is not interested in the job or does not fit the criteria and temperament necessary for effective sponsorship, it might serve both the individual and the organization to find alternative ways for that executive to support the sponsorship program other than serving directly as a sponsor. For executives and senior managers with a desire to serve and an appropriate temperament and basic skill set, a development program to hone their skills and provide support to their sponsorship efforts will serve both the sponsors and the organization and improve the chances of executive and project success. Figure 6.1 represents four focus areas that together provide a foundation for assessing sponsor readiness. First, we look at which sponsors are making a positive contribution to project success, and then we propose evaluating whether the right people are in the sponsor role and if a support mechanism is in place in terms of training and sustainably supporting project management standards. Collectively these elements provide the backdrop for determining sponsor readiness.

Assessment Focus Areas

Project Outcomes and Sponsor Contribution

The goal of sponsorship is to produce successful business outcomes. "Success" might mean bringing a project across the finish line to realize business value or justly terminating a project to minimize losses. Before embarking on a sponsorship improvement initiative, assessing the outcomes of recent projects and the effectiveness of their sponsorship can help determine which aspects of sponsorship are working, which are not,

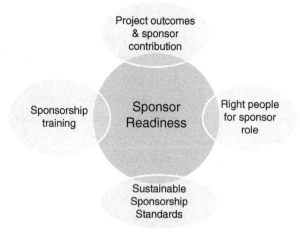

Figure 6.1 Focus areas for sponsorship readiness

and where an improvement program should start. Understanding recent project challenges and failure modes and the underlying causes can inform adjustments to roles, responsibilities, and behavioral criteria.

The first step toward assessing the effectiveness of existing organizational sponsors is building an inventory of recent strategic projects and their outcomes. The criteria suggested in Chapter 2 for determining which projects are candidates for executive sponsorship can be used as a filter to identify a subset of significant projects the organization has completed or cancelled during the previous 2 years. These projects can then be analyzed to establish measures of success. Although purely objective criteria may be inadequate to capture all of the complexities and nuance of real-world project performance, some helpful measures might include:

1. What were the initially established cost, schedule, and scope parameters of the project? If there is no record of the initial project goals, this is a project management and sponsorship issue.
2. What was the initial business case?—If there is no record of the initial business case, this is a project management and sponsorship issue.
3. How did the cost and schedule projections change over time? A simple graph can be created for both cost and schedule that show the history of actual and projected costs and schedule (see Figure 6.2). Significant jumps in cost or schedule should have corresponding change orders or records of issues being identified or addressed that explain what happened and indicate a conscious decision to continue the project.
4. What risks were identified? When were they identified? Which risks occurred? What responses were implemented? How effective were the risk responses?
5. What significant changes were authorized? What were the underlying causes of the changes (e.g., new functionality, changed assumptions, incorrect estimates, changes in resources, externally imposed changes, and so on)?
6. What was the final outcome of the project with respect to its initial business case? In retrospect, was the project a good investment of organizational resources? If not, when was this determined and was it a conscious business decision to continue?

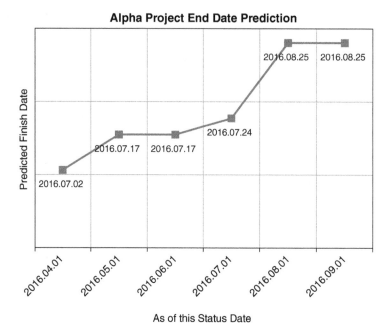

Alpha Project End Date Prediction

Figure 6.2 Example: Graphing schedule performance over time

Graphing Schedule Performance Over Time

This analysis graph is used to show significant variation in a target date. The horizontal axis represents the date the predicted finish was published, and the vertical axis represents the then projected completion. The first prediction was published on April 1 and anticipated a July 2 completion. Four weeks later on May 1, the predicted end date had slipped 15 days to July 17. The following status on June 1 suggested the completion date was unchanged at July 17; however, the July 1 status reflects another slip in the predicted end date to July 24, estimating completion 3 weeks from the status date. The August 1 status predicts an August 25 completion, a surprising four-week slip. Finally, the September 1 status (probably a close-out status report) indicates the project was completed on August 25. When the line moves dramatically on the vertical axis, there should be a corresponding explanation elsewhere in project documentation explaining what happened.

7. What lessons did the team and organization learn from the project? Is there evidence that the lessons learned have been integrated into the organizational culture and applied to other projects?

8. What was the retention rate of the team members during and after the project? Did team members leave the project before it was complete? Did team members leave the organization before the project was complete or within 6 months of project completion?

These questions can generate meaningful information about projects of all shapes and sizes, including those that deliver value and those that are cancelled. For comparison purposes, differences can be expressed as ratios, such as "the project finished 10% over budget." The evidence gathered should provide clues about whether the project was well managed and the effectiveness of the project sponsor.

Taking an inventory of strategic projects and their outcomes provides a basis for assessing not only the executive sponsor but the entire sponsorship program. If an organization has a project closure process that includes criteria for rating project success, that information would also be helpful. If no outcome data are available, then senior management or the Project Management Office (PMO) might be asked to evaluate project successes based on a set of organizationally relevant criteria. Once project success rates are established, each project's sponsor can be assessed on their contribution to the overall project's success.

Subjective assessment of a sponsor's contribution can be accomplished in several ways.

- Ask the sponsor for his or her own perspective on the project. Sponsors will have intimate knowledge of what went well and what did not.
- Solicit input from the project manager. Because they engage in day-to-day interactions with the sponsor, project managers can speak to the fulfillment of roles and responsibility and desirable sponsorship qualities like leadership, support, and responsiveness that influenced project outcomes.
- If the organization has a PMO, ask PMO leadership for their perspective on the project to get an alternative view of the sponsor's influence on project's success.

- Interview key project stakeholders who had a vested interest in the project's outcome; they were likely attuned to sponsorship activities and can share their experiences.

Figure 6.3 depicts the assessment steps outlined above for determining project success rates and sponsor influence on outcomes. Each assessment provides visibility regarding which sponsors are contributing the most to the most successful projects, signaling an action item to determine what these sponsors might be doing that makes them more effective.

Right People for Sponsor Role

If not every executive is suited to serve as a project sponsor, how might an organization determine who is best suited for the role? One approach is to develop a list of sponsorship responsibilities and desired behaviors and then assess your executive team members against that list. As described in Chapter 5, GAPP's *Framework for Performance Based Competency Standards for Project Sponsors*[2] provides an excellent starting point for developing performance criteria as it relates to roles, responsibilities, and expected sponsor behaviors.

In Chapter 5 the focus was on establishing standards for desirable roles, responsibilities, and behaviors, whereas here we focus on determining if the individual is the right person for the role and if so does he or she

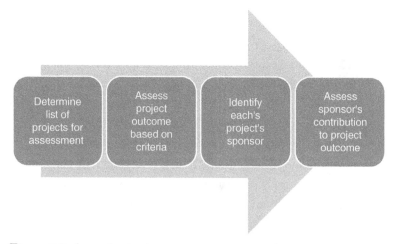

Figure 6.3 Assessing project success outcome and sponsor contribution process

have the skill set to meet expectations of the role. To make this evaluation, consider the following steps:

1. Engage senior management in a discussion about the benefits of sponsorship assessment, such as the identification of sponsorship best practices and skill gaps for personal and professional development.
2. Using the GAPP's standard, review each role, aspects of the responsibilities, and the associated performance goals seen in Table 5.2 in the context of the organization. Seek consensus on tailored criteria for a competency and performance standards model.
3. Once the criteria are finalized, conduct individual senior management interviews with those who have served as sponsors to assess their performance and competency. For those who have not served in the role, the assessment may help to gauge readiness. The scenarios outlined in Chapter 5 provide an opportunity to elicit reactions from the senior management team to hypothetical situations and might generate insightful conversations in places where sponsors disagree or have not thought of some of the broader implications asserted.

The goal of the assessments is not punitive; it is information gathering to establish a foundation for personal improvement. Even so, the proposal to conduct an assessment of individual executives may be met with resistance, so it is important that the organization buy in to the process, understand how it will be used, understand what will be done with the data gathered, and allocate adequate time and resources to conduct the assessments.

Sustainable Sponsorship Standards

Equally important as assessing executive performance and competency is the reviewing and confirming of project management standards for clarifying the sponsor role, responsibilities, and behaviors. For standards to produce the desired results they must meet the current and anticipated needs of the organizational environment in which projects are performed. As role and responsibility needs evolve, mechanisms must be in place to confirm the standard's viability and make any necessary adjustments.

One approach key to keeping standards relevant is to stay abreast of the project management industry's current thinking on sponsorship standards. In Chapter 1, we reviewed the evolution of sponsorship and the sponsor role. During the last 20 years, expectations for the role and responsibilities have changed substantially as more organizations engaged in formal project sponsorship. As the role continues to evolve and be refined, some practical suggestions for keeping current include:

- Monitoring changes to GAPP's standard for sponsorship by checking their site periodically.[3]
- Review Project Management Institute's Project Management Body of Knowledge to understand any updates to the topic of sponsorship.[4]
- Track other reputable project management bodies, such as the International Association of Project Management[5] or Association for Project Management[6], on standards for sponsorship that might provide additional insights for consideration.

These external sources of sponsorship information can be combined with feedback from the executive team to adjust standards for local use. We suggest conducting an annual review of the standards with senior management. This could include a presentation to share emerging industry information regarding sponsorship and a dialogue around recent project experience and perceived changing needs with recommendations regarding how sponsorship standards should adapt. Some questions to stimulate this discussion and identify changing needs include:

- Are the current sponsorship standards providing the desired results? If not, what is not being addressed that would benefit from an adjustment to sponsorship roles and responsibilities?
- What has changed about our project environment that might warrant revising standard sponsor roles, responsibilities, and behaviors? What change would senior management like to see?
- Do the currently defined roles and responsibilities expect too much or too little from sponsors? If so, what might be changed?
- Based on the current rate of project successes, is the sponsorship role as the organization has defined it effective? If not, what would improve it? What standards might be changed?

After collecting input, analyze and recommend changes to the standards. Once senior management has agreed to any refinements, amend the standards, conduct any necessary sponsorship training, and socialize the changes to the organization.

Sponsorship Training

The last step of the sponsorship assessment process is evaluating the scope and effectiveness of existing training support. Figure 6.4 is a graphical representation of a simplified process for determining training gaps and identifying an improvement plan.

Sponsorship is effective when roles, responsibilities, and expected behaviors are understood and sponsors must have an opportunity to discuss these in a setting where learning can occur. Senior managers may reject the assertion that they need training, insisting that they understand what they must do; however, consistent training is necessary for both sponsors and project managers to assure they are hearing the same message and that both have an opportunity to seek clarity on revised standards, expectations, and/or new approaches.

Implementing or refining a sponsorship training program entails determining what training should occur and assessing the effectiveness of existing courses. First, identify training currently provided. This would include both specific

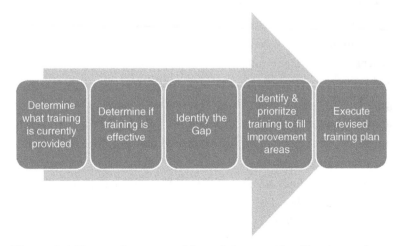

Figure 6.4 Process for sponsorship training gap identification and remediation

project management and sponsorship skills, as well as "soft skills" appropriate to the sponsor role, including negotiation, leadership, and communication.

If no current training is in place for project managers or project sponsors, an initial offering would include at a minimum discussing the sponsor role, responsibilities, and behaviors in the context of standard project management practices, with an emphasis on the sponsor engagement points. Scenario analysis and role-playing are excellent approaches for demonstrating desirable behaviors. One-on-one and customized training may also be appropriate for executives in some instances. Important scenarios to explore include:

- Risk management process with an emphasis on project manager and sponsor interactions
- The project kick-off meeting and corresponding desirable sponsor behaviors (see Table 6.1)
- Change management process
- Issue management process
- Project status reporting

If a sponsor training program exists, determine if it is thorough and effective. Similar to assessing the standards, assess the effectiveness of training by asking participants if they are getting what they need. Ask sponsors and project managers following each training session if the training is meeting their needs. If not, ask what they would like to see more or less of. Periodic surveys sent to sponsors and project managers that solicit anonymous feedback can be another vehicle for gathering information. Other valuable input sources include stakeholders such as senior management and PMO leadership. Performance assessments and project success rates are also useful indicators of possible training gaps. Finally, project retrospectives—reviews of what went well and what needs improvement—can be excellent sources of feedback for training programs. After determining gaps, identify and prioritize training improvement areas.

Delivery methods for training should be appropriate for both the material and the learners. Although experiential learning is often most effective, some subjects may lend themselves to independent study and

Table 6.1 Sponsor roles, responsibilities, and behavior: Project kick-off meeting

Sponsor roles, responsibilities, and behavior Project kick-off meeting	
Desirable behavior	Undesirable alternative
• Sponsor enters the room and stands at the front beside the project manager who is running the meeting • After a welcome by the project manager and review of the agenda, the sponsor is introduced to share his/her view of the project, focusing on its importance to the organization and why he/she is personally glad to be a part of the team • Sponsor stays engaged throughout the kick-off meeting to address any questions from the project team, confirm project manager assertions, and interject where he/she feels it can add value • At the end of meeting, the sponsor thanks the project team for being part of this effort and states they look forward to celebrating at the end this project's successful completion	• Sponsor enters and sits at the front or back of the room and is there for the purpose of answering any questions the project team members might have of him/her • Sponsor has no active role in the meeting • Sponsor does not address the group unless asked a question • Sponsor distracted by cell phone • Sponsor does not stay for entire meeting

some topics may not require formal curricula. Consider the following vehicles when determining how best to deliver sponsorship skills. Each of these methods has advantages and disadvantages (Table 6.2), but whatever delivery mechanism is selected engagement must occur for the message to be heard, internalized, and accepted by the intended audience.

Assessing Sponsor Readiness

After examining the individual components of sponsor readiness above, the next step is assessing the last two components of the framework: training and support (Step 4) and right people in the sponsor role (Step 5).

Table 6.2 Advantages and disadvantages of training delivery methods

Method	Advantage	Disadvantage
Classroom	• Group interaction • Easy-to-ask questions • Learner involvement • Opportunity for role play • Group hears common message	• Rigid time schedule • Time away from job • Instructor quality may vary • Paced for the room, not the individual
Webinar	• Typically shorter time commitment • Typically narrower focus on topic • Allows some questions if real time • When recorded, available on demand	• Rigid time schedule • Largely one-way communication • Engagement is optional • Easy to get distracted, no peer pressure to stay on task • No question opportunities if recorded
Online self-paced	• Self-paced • Facilitates going back to earlier topic when questions arise	• Schedule flexible • Minimal opportunities for questions • Requires discipline to complete
On the job	• Learn as you go from success/failure	• Unstructured learning • No reference material • Individualized message may not be consistent
Mentoring from experienced sponsor	• Customized learning • Individual interaction	• Availability of mentor • Limited reference materials available
Independent study (books, videos, and so on)	• Self-paced • Focused	• If inconsistent sources are used, they must be reconciled for implementation • Requires discipline to complete
Consultant or coach (one-on-one)	• Highly tailored • Can respond to specific requests or situations	• Costly • Does not demonstrate public commitment to learning • Consistency may vary over time with different coaches

Figure 6.5 highlights the fourth and fifth steps in the assessment of the overall health of the sponsorship program.

Referring to the material in this chapter, assess these two areas to identify gaps. Figure 6.4 describes the process steps necessary to determine

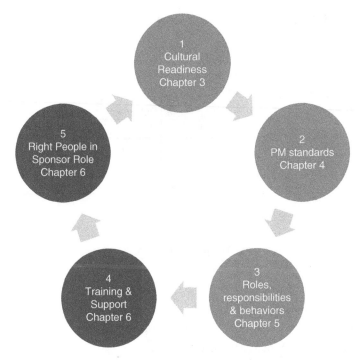

Figure 6.5 Framework for assessing a sponsorship program—training and support and right people in sponsor role focus

whether existing training is effective, where the perceived gaps are, potential solutions to close the gaps, and training solution priorities. Record assessment data in Table 6.3.

Table 6.3 Sponsorship training gap identification and remediation worksheet

Sponsor training provided	Training effectiveness Low 1 ⟷ High 5					Gaps	Potential gap solutions	Training priority H-M-L
	1	2	3	4	5			
	1	2	3	4	5			
	1	2	3	4	5			
	1	2	3	4	5			

Table 6.4 Project success outcomes and sponsor contribution worksheet

Completed strategic projects	Overall project outcome Not met Met 1 ⟵————————⟶ 5		Assigned sponsor	Sponsor contribution to project outcome
	1	2 3 4 5		
	1	2 3 4 5		
	1	2 3 4 5		
	1	2 3 4 5		

To determine whether the right people are being assigned the sponsor role, conduct sponsor interviews to assess their performance and competency and combine that with data gathered on project success and sponsor contribution. Although a project's outcome might not be met because it was canceled, it might still be good sponsorship. Record outcomes and contribution assessment data in Table 6.4.

The results can fuel a discussion with senior management to arrive at consensus scores for step 4 and step 5 of the spider diagram in Figure 7.1. This chapter's exercises provide the final two assessments of the five areas, and establish a baseline for continuous improvement of the sponsorship program explored in Chapter 8.

Discussion Questions

1. Why is executive sponsorship assessment important?
2. Why might some executives resist the suggestion that they should participate in formal assessments or training?
3. Name four focus areas for assessments that provide insight to whether an existing project sponsorship program is meeting its objectives.
4. Who within the organization participates in sponsor assessment, and why?
5. What tools/approach might be useful to determine whether the right person is performing the sponsorship role?

6. Why is an ongoing assessment of the standards for sponsor roles, responsibilities, and behavior critical to the success of the role?

7. What resources are available to keep abreast of changes in the evolving role of the sponsor?

8. Explain the steps in assessing and improving a sponsorship training program. Discuss different approaches and training delivery vehicles and why they might be used.

Considerations

Project Management Office

The PMO has a leadership opportunity to provide insight to senior management regarding sponsor readiness and the strength of the training and project management standards meant to support the sponsors. The PMO can be particularly helpful in collecting, analyzing, synthesizing, and presenting the data for senior management review. In organizations where the PMO is responsible for setting and maintaining standards as well as providing sponsorship training, the PMO can provide an accurate view of current state in terms of training and standards as well as a desired state and rationale from their perspective. In terms of determining if the sponsor is right for the role, the PMO can provide a valuable perspective that should be considered along with other assessment feedback.

Project Manager

Project managers want to promote sponsorship readiness because they benefit from having a fully engaged sponsor who is trained and willing to be a project advocate and mentor. Project managers should seek opportunities to assist in training planning, provide feedback on sponsor engagement, and promote project management standards that encourage collaboration and relationship building between the two roles.

Notes

1. Lewis Carroll. *Alice's Adventures in Wonderland,* (Kindle ed.), (New York: Open Road Integrated, 2014).

2. GAPPS. 2015. A Guiding Framework for Project Sponsors, Sydney, Australia: Global Alliance for Project Performance Standards, accessed October 5, 2015, http://globalpmstandards.org/downloads.
3. GAPPS, 2015.
4. Project Management Institute, accessed October 6, 2015, https://www.pmi.org.
5. International Association of Project Management, accessed October 6, 2015, https://www.iapm.net.
6. Association of Project Management, accessed October 6, 2015, https://apm.org.uk.

CHAPTER 7

Roadmap to Organizational Preparedness

"A goal without a plan is just a wish."

—Antoine de Saint-Exupéry

Our goal for Chapters 1 through 6 was to provide insights into sponsorship to stimulate thinking about improving the effectiveness of sponsorship as a strategic tool. Tangible results of better sponsorship manifest in many ways: increased project successes, improved communications between sponsors and project managers, more timely access to important information, improved decision making, a supportive culture, improved performance, and development and exhibition of better leadership skills from those performing the sponsorship role.

Chapters 3 through 6 described tools and processes for assessing organizational preparedness in the framework component areas. This chapter describes a method for consolidating and displaying assessment information (Figure 7.1) to:

1. Reflect the results of the initial assessment—creating a tool to facilitate initial improvement planning described in the next chapter
2. Support ongoing monitoring and continuous improvement of the sponsorship program once the initial program changes are implemented

The example chart shown here depicts three executive's perceptions of where the organization ranks on a 1–7 scale for each of the five framework

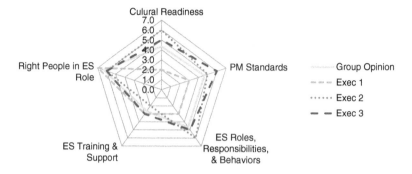

Figure 7.1 Visualizing senior management's perception of organizational preparedness

elements. Also displayed is the group's average response, which might serve as a baseline for improvement. Notice that all three executives believe they have the right people in the executive sponsorship role. There are diverse opinions about where the organization stands on having a supportive culture, project management standards, or clear sponsorship roles and responsibilities. The executives do appear to agree that sponsorship training is lacking. The radar diagram gives an excellent visual of initial attributes needing focus and potential improvement plans.

Tools and Process

The first step in creating the radar diagram involves assessing the five attributes of a sponsorship program: culture readiness, project management standards, sponsor roles and responsibilities, training, and whether the right people are in the sponsor role. After completing the assessments using the assessment tools in Chapters 3 through 6, ask senior management to rate each area using the questionnaire in Table 7.1. Each executive's scores are plotted and the group rating is calculated as the average of the executives scores for each attribute, each executive having equal weight. Attributes that show considerable disparity should be reviewed and discussed to understand the basis for the differing perspectives. The radar diagram then becomes the baseline for measuring and monitoring improvements for sponsorship. If interested in additional viewpoints

Table 7.1 Rating criteria for executive sponsorship program attributes

Rating criteria for Executive Sponsorship program attributes		
Attribute	Score	On a scale from 1 to 7 rank each attribute (1 = Not well 7 = Very well)
Cultural readiness		• How well does our culture support the executive sponsor in this role? (Consider Chapter 3: the 20 questions and Table 3.1)
PM standards		• How well do the project management standards identify sponsor responsibilities? (Consider Chapter 4, Table 4.2)
Executive sponsorship roles and responsibilities		• How well defined and understood are sponsorship roles and responsibilities? (Consider Chapter 5, Tables 5.1 and 5.2)
Executive sponsorship training and support		• How well does sponsorship training provide the sponsor, project manager, and project team with clear roles, responsibilities, and behaviors expected of the executive sponsor role while interacting with the project team and various project stakeholders? (Consider Chapter 6, process Figure 6.4)
Right people in Executive sponsorship role		• How well are the right executives being matched to the right projects requiring sponsorship? (Consider Chapter 6, process Figure 6.3 and Chapter 5, aggregated sponsors performance data to Tables 5.1 and 5.2)

outside the executive team, two more scores could be added: one representing Project Management Office (PMO) leadership and a second representing a group of senior-level project managers. If their scores are radically different than the executive scores, further discussion and consideration for improvement priorities might be warranted.

Baseline Assessment

Although the assessment inputs from the chapters may be sufficient for making initial organizational preparedness rating decisions, the questionnaire (Table 7.1) may help facilitate further discussion to gain executive

How to Set Up a Radar Diagram in a Spreadsheet

The radar diagram requires no special software and can be created using a spreadsheet application, for example, Microsoft Excel 2010 from the Microsoft Office suite of products. To do this, open up Excel, click on the INSERT tab, click on the "Other Charts" icon, and select one of three Radar diagram formats. Set up the excel table with the first column as the sponsorship program elements, the second column as "Group Opinion," and the third, fourth, and so on columns with the names of the executives completing this exercise. The rows represent the five radar diagram attributes where scores are entered for each executive on each of the attribute. Label the rows accordingly: Cultural Readiness, PM Standards, Executive sponsorship Roles and Responsibilities, Executive sponsorship Training & Support, and Right People in Executive sponsorship role. Enter the scores for each executive on each of the five attributes into the spreadsheet and generate the radar diagram. Use the "Average" function to aggregate all executive scores for each attribute to create the Group Opinion score. Other computer and cloud-based spreadsheet applications provide similar functionality.

perspectives. The questionnaire summarizes the assessment criteria used for rating each attribute, taking into consideration chapter material and tools. Each assessment tool is listed for easy reference.

When ratings have been performed and recorded, review the results and identify which attributes offer the best opportunities for improvement. This will be input to improvement planning in Chapter 8.

Senior management dialogue about an organization's preparedness to support executive sponsorship is healthy. It provides an opportunity for debate among senior management regarding what has worked well, what has not, and how and when organizational change should occur. It provides the forum to discuss selection criteria for sponsors, expected roles, responsibilities, and behavior, and improvements for development and support. It provides a forum for executives to express their opinions and shape the role.

Ongoing Monitoring and Continuous Improvement

We recommend making continuous sponsorship improvement a strategic initiative. The same radar chart can be used to track progress for the initiative by periodically reassessing each attribute and producing an updated radar diagram. The visible evolution of preparedness to support executive sponsorship provides an opportunity to demonstrate improvement and the effectiveness of efforts to date while guiding planning for future enhancements.

Discussion Questions

1. Why are soliciting individual senior management perspectives on the five sponsorship program attributes important?
2. How can continuous improvement of sponsorship become a strategic initiative?
3. Why is a radar diagram a good tool for senior management's use in monitoring progress?
4. How might input from the PMO or project managers be integrated into the assessment?

Considerations

Project Management Office

The PMO can play a pivotal role by facilitating the operational preparedness meeting. Not only does facilitation provide a leadership opportunity to guide and shape the plan but it promotes additional value that the PMO can offer. The insight gained as to the gaps to be filled provides opportunities for new roles the PMO can play for adding value.

Project Manager

The project manager should use the operational preparedness assessment to identify ways he or she can make significant contributions to the improvement efforts. Be it leading an improvement team, designing new standards and processes, or facilitating training sessions, the project manager has an opportunity to practice and showcase his or her leadership, negotiation, communication, and teamwork skills. Use these occasions to become visible and further develop your network.

CHAPTER 8

A Plan to Enhance Executive Sponsorship

> "All things are created twice; first mentally; then physically. The key to creativity is to begin with the end in mind, with a vision and a blue print of the desired result"
>
> —Stephen Covey

This chapter describes a process (Figure 8.1) for integrating ideas and information gathered from prior chapters into an overall plan for developing or improving an executive sponsorship program. We strongly recommend performing an initial assessment of all five areas of the sponsorship framework (Figure 1.1) using the assessment tools from Chapters 3 through 6 and working with the executive team to obtain baseline metrics about an organization's current state of sponsorship to support an integrated and holistic approach to planning improvements.

Although the book's design supports choosing one or more components that need attention and dealing with them individually, this can be risky if implementation planning does not consider the support structures that must exist to sustain improvements implemented in isolation. For example, if sponsor roles, responsibilities, and expected behaviors have not previously been established and agreed upon, then creating a sponsor training program would be a futile exercise.

Building the Plan

The steps outlined below offer a systems approach to process improvement. The goal is to build support for the program incrementally with

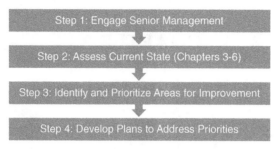

Figure 8.1 *Process for building sponsorship improvement plan*

small focused victories, rather than trying to attain commitment to build and implement a large and unwieldy plan that cannot be responsive to local culture and the facts on the ground. A flexible implementation of agreed upon priorities will help build and sustain momentum for the process improvements necessary to successfully build an executive sponsorship program.

The Plan—Step 1: Engage Senior Management

The key to successfully designing and implementing an improved executive sponsorship program is senior management engagement. Two kinds of engagement and commitment are required:

1. General support for the sponsorship improvement initiative—Senior management must understand the value of effective project management and executive sponsorship to the organization and be willing to commit the time and resources needed to implement improvements long enough to see results. Organizational change is hard, and an executive sponsorship initiative requires sustained commitment. While some near-term improvements might demonstrate value, it could be 9 months to a year or more before isolated successes can be recognized as positive trends that impact the project outcomes, so senior management needs to be willing to stay the course.
2. Explicit support for specific efforts to improve sponsorship—The general support referenced above gains agreement for the journey to improve sponsorship. Explicit support is about gaining agreement

and commitment to the proposed steps to reach that goal. Explicit support will be facilitated by seeking incremental agreement to a series of modest improvements that will be selected and prioritized in consultation with the senior management team.

Achieving engagement and general commitment to the effort is the essential first step. Chapter 2 provided information about the value of sponsorship to help build a case for the necessary support. The two fundamental questions the senior management team should consider are:

- "Do we believe there is room for improvement in our strategic project performance?"
- "Do we believe an investment in better executive sponsorship would contribute to that improvement?"

If both answers are affirmative this should translate into the organizational will to initiate and support the sponsorship improvement effort. If either answer is no, the organization is not ready to support a sponsorship initiative.

Support for specific improvement efforts will be developed more slowly and be built over time. Senior management will be involved in the assessments described in Chapters 3 through 6 and the prioritization and planning for improvements. That participation should help build the necessary commitment for explicit improvement plans.

The Plan—Step 2: Assess Current State (Chapters 3–6)

In consultation with senior management, determine which assessment tools might provide the best insights into the current state of the organization. Perform the assessments and identify gaps and opportunities for improvement. Table 8.1 recaps the assessment tools shared in Chapters 3 through 6 and the corresponding material provides background for each assessment.

Assembling data from each assessment component in the framework (Figure 1.1) helps the sponsorship improvement team gauge initial organizational preparedness and establish a baseline for process improvement.

Table 8.1 Recap of sponsorship assessment tools

Location	Assessment tools
Chapter 3 Table 3.1	• 20 cultural questions • Cultural behaviors/orientation related to project management worksheet
Table 4.2	• Standardized process for sponsor involvement worksheet
Table 5.1 Table 5.2	• Summary of roles, responsibilities, and performance criteria worksheet • Desired behavior and temperaments worksheet
Table 6.3 Table 6.4	• Sponsorship training gap identification and remediation worksheet • Project success outcomes and sponsor contribution worksheet

Chapter 7, Figure 7.1 presents a visualization tool for these assessment data that is helpful for communication and monitoring ongoing improvements.

The Plan—Step 3: Identify and Prioritize Areas for Improvement

When analysis results are available, share the findings with senior management and identify and prioritize areas for improvement. While individual organizations may have unique constraints or challenges requiring special consideration, we recommend a holistic approach inform the prioritization process. Some process improvements have prerequisite infrastructure requirements and inter-relationships or interactions with other elements that must be considered as part of prioritization. The framework for assessing a sponsorship program also suggests a sequence for process improvement. For example, if an organization is assessed to have a low cultural readiness score and a low PM standards score, experience suggests that addressing and improving cultural readiness first will usually be most productive, putting in place the necessary cultural support for later standards enhancement. Table 8.2 identifies the recommended priorities for consideration in each of the assessment framework components.

Once all priority 1 items requiring attention have been addressed, Table 8.3 identifies the priority 2 items that would represent the next priorities for consideration.

When all priority 1 and priority 2 items have been addressed, Table 8.4 identifies the priority 3 items that would round out the foundation of an executive sponsorship program.

Table 8.2 Recommended first-priority gaps/weaknesses to address (if present)

Assessment framework component	Priority 1—gap/weakness to address
Cultural (see Table 3.1)	• Blaming • Embrace process • Response to risk • Business orientation
PM standards (Table 1.1, Table 4.1, Figures 4.2– 4.5)	• Project life-cycle processes with associated sponsor engagement points • Communication Package • Meeting Minute Package • Risk management process • Change control process • Charter
Enterprise sponsor roles, responsibilities, and behaviors (Figure 5.1, Table 5.1)	• 6 behaviors and temperaments adopted (Figure 5.1) • GAPPS' 3 roles and 10 responsibilities adopted (Table 5.1)
Training and support (corresponds to priorities above)	• Project management standards • Sponsorship roles, responsibilities, behaviors and temperaments
Right people in sponsor role	• Sponsor assessment criteria defined— match this to the enterprise sponsor roles, responsibilities, and behaviors above

Table 8.3 Recommended second-priority gaps/weaknesses to address (if present)

Assessment framework component	Priority 2—gap/weakness to address
Cultural (see Table 3.1)	• Collaboration • Executive transparency • Theory X/Y
PM standards (Figure 2.1)	• Project prioritization for sponsorship process
Enterprise sponsor roles, responsibilities, and behaviors (Table 5.1)	• Performance criteria for each of the responsibilities (see GAPPS' suggestions Table 5.1)
Training and support (corresponds to priorities above)	• Education to support each of the 3 role groupings/10 responsibilities of the GAPPS framework
Right people in sponsor role	• Sponsors assessments conducted

Table 8.4 Recommended third-priority gaps/weaknesses to address (if present)

Assessment framework component	Priority 3—gap/weakness to address
Cultural (see Table 3.1)	• Flexibility and adaptability
PM standards (Figures 2.2 and 2.3)	• Nomination form for project sponsorship (Figure 2.3) • Executive sponsorship assignment process (Figure 2.2)
Enterprise sponsor roles, responsibilities, and behaviors (Table 5.1)	• Reviewing roles, responsibilities, behavior, and temperaments for applicability and changes implemented
Training and support (corresponds to priorities above)	• Giving constructive feedback and self-reflection on personal development • Project review lessons learned integrated into training
Right people in sponsor role	• Professional development/action plans formally developed and performance monitored

After preliminary prioritization is complete, small logical groups of prioritized items can then move on to more detailed planning. Collections should be assembled with consideration for interdependencies and support structures. For example, if the need to improve change control processes were identified as a priority gap, developing and providing training to socialize and reinforce the new standard would be a strong candidate for the same effort.

The Plan—Step 4: Develop Plans to Address Priorities

Small collections of the prioritized items from Step 3 above are now fed iteratively into the planning process. Solutions appropriate to the organization's context and maturity must be identified and plans formulated to address these priorities. As mentioned in Chapter 1, we believe the secret to successfully implementing a sponsorship improvement initiative, or any significant organizational change effort, is to plan for modest incremental improvements. The goal is to build a series of cohesive and actionable plans. Each plan should represent the minimum change necessary to address and support one or two of the identified priorities and be implementable in 2–4 months so that results are visible and momentum can be sustained. The most effective plans will include mechanisms for feedback and ongoing refinement and process improvement.

Sample Action Plan

Gap: Sponsor training needs improvement

1. Form an action team of executive sponsors, PMO staff, project managers, and training department personnel to perform this sponsor training program update
2. Determine and prioritize learning objectives/topics to be improved/added in this iteration
3. Review existing training courses for quality and applicability
4. Develop a list of training solutions to address identified topics
5. Review proposed solutions with senior management and gain buy-in and approval
6. Secure trainers, courses, methods of delivery
7. Conduct pilot training
8. Adjust training solutions and curriculum based on participant feedback
9. Implement and standardize training program
10. Report results to senior management team
11. Monitor participation (who attends) and participant feedback (were objectives met) and report results regularly until the program has been institutionalized and is stable
12. Modify performance criteria to incorporate training outcomes and assess if new practices or roles, responsibilities, and behaviors are being practiced.

Implementing a series of changes to address priority topics will move the organization toward the goal of improved executive sponsorship. Small steps show progress, build momentum, and allow for the occasional misstep without undermining confidence in the overall effort. A holistic approach for developing improvement plans helps the organization recognize and respond to the interconnectivity among the five components of the framework. Effective prioritization helps avoid weakness in one component undermining improvement efforts in another area.

Planning for Continuous Improvement

Once implementation of improvement plans begins, the material in Chapter 7 provides a tool to help visualize and monitor progress at an organizational level. At a more tactical level, there are several performance measures (Table 8.5) that can help confirm that the improvement plans are progressing and achieving their desired outcomes.

Refining executive sponsorship is a journey, not a destination. Ongoing monitoring of:

- Organizational culture
- Effectiveness and fit of local project management standards
- Continuing evolution of sponsor roles and responsibilities and patterns of behavior
- Effectiveness of training and mentoring programs
- Project outcomes

provides information about areas needing renewed focus and previous solutions that need further refinement. PMOs are often well situated to perform this monitoring and present the results to senior management, as well as taking the lead in ongoing improvement efforts.

Summary

Building improvement plans for each of the components of the framework need not be complicated, but it does require a thoughtful, co-ordinated effort and involvement from key stakeholders in the sponsorship program. Chapter 7 explores the creation of the organization preparedness diagram to aid in developing a holistic approach to prioritizing the areas that need attention first and provides a mechanism for ongoing progress monitoring as improvement plans are implemented.

Table 8.5 Measures of progress toward achieving framework goals

Assessment framework component	Priority level	Ways to measure
Cultural	P1, P2, P3 P1, P2, P3 P1, P2, P3 P1, P2, P3	• Evidence-based assessment performed • Improvement plan documented • Improvement plan executed • Improvement assessment performed
PM standards	P1 P2 P3	• Evidence that the five basic standards, tools, and processes are being consistently developed and used on all significant projects • Evidence that project prioritization process exists and is being used to determine which projects should have executive sponsors assigned • Evidence that a sponsor nomination and assignment process exists and is being used
Executive sponsor roles, responsibilities, and behaviors	P1 P2 P3 P1 P3	• Evidence of GAPPS roles and responsibilities in place • Performance criteria developed and approved for each of the GAPPS roles and responsibilities • Evidence that sponsor performance is being assessed using the GAPPS framework • Evidence of assessment of the six behaviors/temperaments • Evidence that role and responsibility reviews and continuous improvements are being conducted and implemented
Training and support	P1 P1 P2 P3	• The availability of training that focuses on project management standards • The availability of training that focuses on sponsor roles, responsibilities, and expected behaviors • Evidence of participation in that training by all sponsors • Evidence that the training is being continually assessed for effectiveness
Right people in sponsor role	P1 P2 P3	• Evidence that professional development/action plans for executives include sponsorship responsibilities • Evidence that sponsor assessments are being routinely performed for all sponsors • Evidence that action plans are being developed and implemented to address any identified deficiencies and that results are being monitored

Discussion Questions

1. What benefit(s) are there to using a systems approach for determining a holistic improvement plan for the sponsorship program?
2. What benefits are there to having a holistic view of the sponsorship program?
3. What challenges can you imagine encountering when trying to establish an executive sponsorship improvement program? How might they be addressed?

Considerations

Project Management Office

The PMO benefits by leading and managing the sponsorship program improvement plans. There is an opportunity to build relationships with senior management team members by providing coaching and improved standardized processes and tools[1] that assist them in performing their sponsor roles more effectively. The PMO also benefits from more effective sponsors by producing more successful projects with fewer issues. PMO staff can offer insight into the inter-relationships among the different focus areas and will likely have a more pragmatic view of the current state of organizational preparedness. PMO recommendations about the sequence of action plan implementation can be valuable input to the management team.

Project Manager

Project managers and the organization both benefit from project manager participation in gap identification and improvement teams. This provides project managers an opportunity to converse with executives about their needs and demonstrate leadership and problem-solving skills. Project managers play a key part in educating executives about the sponsorship role and the competencies necessary to be a great sponsor. In return, project managers benefit from increased chances of being assigned a skilled sponsor that better meets project needs.[2]

Notes

1. Vicki James, Ron Rosenhead, and Peter Taylor, P. 2013. Strategies for Project Sponsorship, (Tysons Corner, VA: Management Concepts), p. 164.
2. James, Rosenhead, and Taylor, 2013. p. 160.

CHAPTER 9

Summary

"In literature and in life we ultimately pursue, not conclusions, but beginnings."

—Sam Tanenhaus[1]

Much like Sam Tanenhuaus's quote about conclusions, reading this summary is not the end but just the beginning of a journey for leveraging sponsorship as a strategic tool. We have tried to establish a foundation for why sponsorship matters and provide tools for assessing an organization's current state and building a sponsorship improvement plan; the next steps rely on taking action. This entails engaging in dialogue about the health of your sponsorship program and exploring how to make sponsorship more effective.

Additional Benefits of Sponsorship

Throughout the book the emphasis has been on using executive sponsorship strategically to deliver successful projects. In Chapter 2, we emphasize leveraging sponsorship as a leadership development tool across several levels of the organization. What is not explored is leveraging executive sponsorship as an external strategic tool, with clients or suppliers to drive more business, strengthen relationships, and build stronger partnerships. There are a number of opportunities for effective sponsorship to benefit an organization externally. As an example, well-executed, externally facing projects with effective executive sponsorship engagement demonstrate the commitment an organization has to ensuring project successes to external constituents. This action alone exudes good will and aids in building trust and healthy relationships. This topic could be another chapter or even a book in itself.

Take-Away Messages

There are several take-away messages we would like to leave you with, as a book is only as good as the value it brings its readers.

Take-Away Message #1: Evolving Good to Great

We hope that by examining and improving how an organization engages in sponsorship, it can evolve from good to great,[2] from doing an adequate job to doing a superior job in delivering successful projects. Successful projects are a competitive advantage for all organizations, reducing waste and improving quality, delivery time, and cost efficiency. Whether your executives are self-taught or formally trained sponsors, there are opportunities for improvement of senior management, Project Management Office leaders, and project managers in strengthening their sponsorship program. If sponsor roles and responsibilities are not on par with the recently released Global Alliance for Project Performance sponsorship standards, or an organization does not currently assess sponsors to determine if they are modeling the behaviors and roles as expected, there are opportunities for improvement. Creating a plan for improvement is worth the time invested if it will produce more successful projects, better leaders, stronger project managers, and enhanced client and supplier relationships.

Take-Away Message # 2: Great Management Lessons Apply

Some of the lessons from the great management books of the past 25 years apply to sponsorship. For instance in Michael Porter's *Competitive Advantage: Creating and Sustaining Superior Performance,* the emphasis is on analyzing the value chain to identify what creates value and causes the product or service to be differentiated.[3] We believe effective sponsorship is a differentiator that creates value because it influences the delivery of successful projects. We contend that with the proper environment and formalized standards, roles, responsibilities, and training, sponsors can be more effective in executing their roles thereby leading to more successful project outcomes. It is prudent, therefore, to investigate the health of your project sponsorship program and determine gaps where improvements can be made with the intent that these improvements will increase the likelihood of project success.

In Peter Senge's *The Fifth Discipline: The Art & Practice of The Learning Organization,* the author contends that organizations survive and thrive by becoming "learning organizations."[4] Our message is, don't succumb to "skilled incompetence, in which people in groups grow incredibility efficient at keeping themselves from learning."[5] Use examination of the sponsorship program as an opportunity to shift the mindset of the executive management team and find more effective roles, responsibilities, and behavior that bring desired results. Require sponsor training and leverage sponsor assessments to ensure newly introduced tools, techniques, and processes are understood and being modeled.

Finally, in John P. Kotter's *Leading Change,* he maintains that organizations fail to change because they fail at altering behavior.[6] If an organization is seeking changes in sponsorship then it must focus on the behaviors it wants executives to model. We argued that if senior managers walked-the-talk then they would influence how others supported sponsorship. We maintained that if an organization expects certain desirable sponsor behaviors then it must assess sponsors and be willing to take corrective action for nonperformance in order to alter those behaviors. Chapter 5 highlights six desirable behaviors and temperaments: communicating effectively, handling ambiguity, managing self, and being responsive, collaborative, and approachable. These are essential to effective sponsorship, and leadership in general.

Take-Away Message #3: Call to Action

Improving executive sponsorship is more likely to be achievable when senior leaders believe it is worth the investment of their time. That is not to say a bottom-up approach cannot work, but our experience says the top-down support garners the most momentum and provides the best opportunity for lasting change.

Treat the sponsorship initiative as a strategic project—charter it, understand the stakeholders, establish a plan, execute the plan, monitor activities, control the quality of the outcomes, and close each phase. Use the framework for building or improving a sponsorship program to guide your plan. Pick the tools that address specific weaknesses and use them as is or customize to fit local needs. If there is room for improvement and potential benefit from investing the time to make enhancements, the key first step is engaging senior management in discussion. As talks progress and interest is solidified, initiate a sponsorship enhancement project and begin the journey.

Closing Thoughts

We hope you have found this book insightful and that it will be useful as a reference in the future. We welcome opportunities to hear about your sponsorship challenges, successes, or questions as well as your experiences using or building upon the ideas we have presented.

Dr. Dawne E. Chandler, PMP
dawnechandler@gmail.com

Payson Hall, PMP
Payson@catalysisgroup.com

Notes

1. Sam Tanenhaus. 1986. *Literature Unbound,* (New York, NY: Ballantine Books).
2. James C. Collins. 2001. *Good to Great: Why Some Companies Make the Leap-and Others Don't,* (New York, NY: HarperBusiness).
3. Michael E. Porter. 1998. *The Competitive Advantage: Creating and Sustaining Superior Performance,* (Republished with a new introduction, 1998), (New York, NY: The Free Press).
4. Peter M. Senge. 1990. *The Fifth Discipline: The Art & Practice of The Learning Organization,* (New York, NY: Doubleday).
5. Senge, 1990, p. Book jacket.
6. John P. Kotter. 1996. *Leading Change,* (Boston, MA: Harvard Business School Press).

References

Association of Project Management. 2016. Accessed October 6, 2015. https://apm.org.uk.

Aubry, Monique, and Brian Hobbs. 2011. "A Fresh Look at the Contribution of Project Management to Organizational Performance." *Project Management Journal, 42*(1):3–16. doi:10.1002/pmj.20213.

Blomquist, Tomas, and Ralph Müller. 2006. "Practices, Roles, and Responsibilities of Middle Managers in Program and Portfolio Management." *Project Management Journal, 37*(1):52–66.

Bodell, Lisa. May 15, 2012. "5 Ways Process Is Killing Your Productivity." *Fast Company*. Accessed July 17, 2016. http://www.fastcompany.com/1837301/5-ways-process-killing-your-productivity.

Bryde, David James. 2003. "Modelling Project Management Performance." *The International Journal of Quality & Reliability Management, 20*(2/3):228–253.

Bryde, David. 2008. "Perceptions of the Impact of Project Sponsorship Practices on Project Success." *International Journal of Project Management, 26*(8):800–809. doi:10.1016/j.ijproman.2007.12.001.

Carroll, Lewis. 2014. *Alice's Adventures in Wonderland*. Kindle ed. New York, NY: Open Road Integrated Media.

Chandler, Dawne E. 2013. "The Relationship Between Senior Management's Perception of the Sustainability of Project Management Value and the Executive Sponsorship Role." PhD dissertation, Capella University. ProQuest Dissertations & Thesis (PQDT). (3600916).

Chandler, Dawne, and Janice L. Thomas. 2015. "Does Executive Sponsorship Matter for Realizing Project Management Value?" *Project Management Journal, 46*(5):46–61. doi:10.1002/pmj.21521.

Christenson, Dale, and Janice Christenson. 2010. "*Fundamentals of Project Sponsorship*." Paper presented at the 2010 PMI Global Congress Proceedings, Washington, DC. Retrieved from http://www.pmi.org.

Collins, James. C. 2001. *Good to Great: Why Some Companies Make the Leap-and Others Don't*. New York, NY: HarperBusiness.

Cooke-Davies, Terrence J. 2005. "*The Executive Sponsor: The Hinge Upon Which Organizational Project Management Maturity Turns?*" Paper presented at the 2005 PMI Global Congress Proceedings, Edinburgh, Scotland. Retrieved from http://www.pmi.org.

Cooke-Davies, T., Crawford, L., Hobbs, B., Labuschagne, L., & Remington, K. 2006. *"Exploring the role of the executive sponsor."* Paper presented at the PMI Research Conference 2006, Montreal, Quebec. Retrieved from http://www.pmi.org

Cooke-Davies, Terry, Svetlana Cicmil, Lynn Crawford, and Kurt Richardson. 2007. "We're Not in Kansas Anymore, Toto: Mapping the Strange Landscape of Complexity Theory, and its Relationship to Project Management." *Project Management Journal, 38*(2):50–61.

Crawford, L., Pollack, J., & England, D. (2006). "Uncovering the trends in project management: Journal emphases over the last 10 years." *International Journal of Project Management, 24*(2), 175 – 184. doi:10.1016/j.ijproman.2005.10.005

Crawford, Lynn, Terry Cooke-Davies, Brian Hobbs, Les Labuschagne, Kaye Remington, and Ping Chen. 2008a. "Governance and Support in the Sponsoring of Projects and Programs." *Project Management Journal, 39*(1):S43–S55. doi:10.1002/pmj.20059.

Crawford, Lynn, Terry Cooke-Davies, Brian Hobbs, Les Labuschagne, Kaye Remington, and Ping Chen. 2008b. *Situational Sponsorship of Projects and Programs: An Empirical Review.* Newtown Square, PA: Project Management Institute.

Englund, Randall. L., and Alfonso Bucero. 2015. *Project Sponsorship: Achieving Management Commitment for Project Success.* 2nd ed. Newtown Square, PA: Project Management Institute.

GAPPS. 2015. *A Guiding Framework for Project Sponsors.* Sydney, Australia: Global Alliance for Project Performance Standards. Accessed October 5, 2015. http://globalpmstandards.org/downloads.

Gawande, Atul. 2009. *The Checklist Manifesto: How to Get Things Right.* New York, NY: Metropolitan Books.

Hall, Mark, Robin Holt, and David Purchase. 2003. "Project Sponsors Under New Public Management: Lessons From the Frontline." *International Journal of Project Management, 21*(7):495–502. doi:10.1016/S0263-7863(02)00054-6.

Helm, Jane, and Kaye Remington. 2005. "Effective Project Sponsorship: An Evaluation of the Role of the Executive Sponsor in Complex Infrastructure Projects by Senior Project Managers." *Project Management Journal, 36*(3):51–61.

Hydari, Huma. 2012. "Project Sponsorship: An Essential Guide for Those Sponsoring Projects Within Their Organizations by David West [Book review]." *Project Management Journal, 43*(1):93–93. doi:10.1002/pmj.20287.

International Association of Project Managers. 2016. Accessed October 6, 2015. https://www.iapm.net.

James, Vicki M. 2011. *"Project Sponsorship: A Collaborative Journey."* Paper presented at the 2011 PMI Global Congress Proceedings, Dallas, TX. Retrieved from http://www.pmi.org

James, Vicki, Ron Rosenhead, and Peter Taylor. 2013. *Strategies for Project Sponsorship*. Tysons Corner, VA: Management Concepts.

Kerzner, Harold. 2004. *Advanced Project Management: Best Practices on Implementation*. 2nd ed. Hoboken, NJ: John Wiley & Sons.

Kloppenborg, Timothy J. 2012. "*Twenty-First Century Project Success Measures: Evolution, Interpretation, Direction*." Paper presented at the PMI° Research and Education Conference, Limerick, Ireland. Retrieved from http://www.pmi.org.

Kloppenborg, Timothy J., and Lawrence J. Laning. 2012. *Strategic Leadership of Portfolio and Project Management*. New York, NY: Business Expert Express.

Kloppenborg, Timothy J., Chris Manolis, and Debbie Tesch. 2009. "Successful Project Sponsor Behaviors During Project Initiation: An Empirical Investigation." *Journal of Managerial Issues, 21*(1):140–159. Retrieved from http://www.pittstate.edu/department/economics/journal-of-managerial-issues/.

Kloppenborg, Timothy J., Debbie Tesch, and Ravi Chinta. 2010. "*Demographic Determinants of Project Success Behaviors*." Paper presented at the PMI Research and Education Conference, Washington, D.C. Retrieved from http://www.pmi.org.

Kloppenborg, Timothy J., Debbie Tesch, and Chris Manolis. 2011. "Investigation of the Sponsor's Role in Project Planning." *Management Research Review, 34*(4):400–416. doi:10.1108/01409171111117852.

Kloppenborg, Timothy J., Debbie Tesch D., Chris Manolis, and Mark Heitkamp. 2006. "An Empirical Investigation of the Sponsor's Role in Project Initiation." *Project Management Journal, 37*(3):16–25.

Kotter, John. P. 1996. *Leading Change*. Boston, MA: Harvard Business School Press.

Kozak-Holland, Mark. 2011. *The History of Project Management*. Oshawa, ON, Canada: Multi-Media Publications.

Labuschagne, Les, Terry Cooke-Davies, Lynn Crawford, Brian Hobbs, and Kaye Remington. 2006. "*Exploring the Role of the Project Sponsor*." Paper presented at the 2006 PMI Global Congress Proceedings, Seattle, WA. Retrieved from http://www.pmi.org.

Theory X and Theory Y. 2016. "NetMBA Business Knowledge Center." Accessed May 22, 2016. http://www.netmba.com/mgmt/ob/motivation/mcgregor/.

Padar, Katalin, Bela Pataki, and Zoltan Sebestyen. 2011. "A Comparative Analysis of Stakeholder and Role Theories in Project Management and Change Management." *International Journal of Management Cases, 13*(4):252–260.

Pinto, Jeffrey K. 2000. "Understanding the Role of Politics in Successful Project Management." *International Journal of Project Management, 18*(2):85–91. doi:10.1016/s0263-7863(98)00073-8.

Porter, Michael E. 1998. *The Competitive Advantage: Creating and Sustaining Superior Performance.* (Republished with a new introduction, 1998). New York, NY: The Free Press.

Project Management Institute. 2000. *A Guide to the Project Management Body of Knowledge (PMBOK guide).* 2000 ed. Newtown Square, PA: Author.

Project Management Institute. 2007. *Project Manager Competency Development Framework.* 2nd ed. Newtown Square, PA: Author.

Project Management Institute. 2013. *A Guide to the Project Management Body of Knowledge (PMBOK guide).* 5th ed. Newtown Square, PA: Author.

Project Management Institute. 2015b. *PMI'S Pulse of the Profession: Capturing the Value of Project Management.* Newtown Square, PA: Author.

Project Management Institute. 2016. *PMI's Pulse of the Profession: The High Cost of Low Performance.* Newtown Square, PA: Author, p.13.

Senge, Peter. 1990. *The Fifth Discipline: The Art & Practice of the Learning Organization.* New York, NY: Doubleday.

Sense, Andrew J. 2013. "A Project Sponsor's Impact on Practice-Based Learning within Projects." *International Journal of Project Management, 31*(2):264–271. doi:10.1016/j.ijproman.2012.06.007.

Sewchurran, Kosheck, and Michelle Barron. 2008. "An Investigation into Successfully Managing and Sustaining the Project Sponsor-Project Manager Relationship Using Soft Systems Methodology." *Project Management Journal, 3*:S56–S68. doi:10.1002/pmj.20060.

Syed, Matthew. 2015. *Black Box Thinking: Why Most People Never Learn From Their Mistakes — But Some Do.* New York, NY: Penguin Random House.

Tanenhaus, Sam. 1986. *Literature Unbound.* New York, NY: Ballantine Books.

Tighe, Gary. 1998. "From Experience: Securing Sponsors and Funding for New Product Development Projects—The Human Side of Enterprise." *Journal of Product Innovation Management, 15*(1):75–81. doi:10.1016/S0737-6782(97)00069-6.

Walker, Derek, and Christopher Dart. 2011. Frontinus: A Project Manager From the Roman Empire Era. *Project Management Journal, 42*(5):4–16. doi:10.1002/pmj.20253.

Weinberg, Gerald M. 1991. *Quality Software Management Volume 3: Congruent Action.* New York, NY: Dorset House.

West, David. 2010. *Project Sponsorship: An Essential Guide for Those Sponsoring Projects Within Their Organizations,* 15–21. Burlington, VT: Gower Publishing Company.

Whitten, Neal. 2002. "Duties of the Effective Project Sponsor." *PM Network.* Retrieved from http://www.pmi.org.

Wright, J. Nevan. 1997. "Time and Budget: The Twin Imperatives of a Project Sponsor." *International Journal of Project Management, 15*(3):181–186. doi:10.1016/S0263-7863(96)00059-2.

Index

OTHER TITLES IN OUR PORTFOLIO AND PROJECT MANAGEMENT COLLECTION

Timothy J. Kloppenborg, *Editor*

- *Making Projects Sing: A Musical Perspective of Project Management* by Raji Sivaraman and Chris Wilson
- *Agile Project Management for Business Transformation Success* by Milan Frankl and Paul Paquette
- *Leveraging Business Analysis for Project Success* by Vicki James
- *Project Portfolio Management: A Model for Improved Decision Making* by Clive N. Enoch
- *Project Management Essentials* by Kathryn Wells and Timothy J. Kloppenborg
- *The Agile Edge: Managing Projects Effectively Using Agile Scrum* by Brian Vanderjack
- *Project Teams: A Structured Development Approach* by Vittal S. Anantatmula
- *Attributes of Project-Friendly Enterprises* by Vittal S. Anantatmula and Parviz F. Rad
- *Stakeholder-led Project Management: Changing the Way We Manage Projects* by Louise Worsley
- *Innovative Business Projects: Breaking Complexities, Building Performance, Volume One: Fundamentals and Project Environment* by Rajagopal
- *KNOWledge SUCCESSion: Sustained Performance and Capability Growth Through Strategic Knowledge Projects* by Arthur Shelley

Announcing the Business Expert Press Digital Library

Concise e-books business students need for classroom and research

This book can also be purchased in an e-book collection by your library as

- a one-time purchase,
- that is owned forever,
- allows for simultaneous readers,
- has no restrictions on printing, and
- can be downloaded as PDFs from within the library community.

Our digital library collections are a great solution to beat the rising cost of textbooks. E-books can be loaded into their course management systems or onto students' e-book readers. The **Business Expert Press** digital libraries are very affordable, with no obligation to buy in future years. For more information, please visit **www.businessexpertpress.com/librarians**. To set up a trial in the United States, please email **sales@businessexpertpress.com**.

CPSIA information can be obtained
at www.ICGtesting.com
Printed in the USA
LVHW041827291020
670187LV00011B/1103